SheBreathes
SOUL STORIES

FROM TRIUMPH TO TRANSFORMATION

How 22 Women Reclaimed Their Joy

Inspired and Curated By:

JENNIFER GULBRAND

GODDESS GLOW PUBLISHING

Copyright ©2023 by Jennifer Gulbrand

Published by Goddess Glow Publishing

Designed & Created in the USA

First Printing, 2023

ISBN - 979-8-9877559-2-1

eBook ISBN - 979-8-9877559-3-8

Library of Congress Cataloguing in Publication Date

Names: Jennifer Gulbrand, Author

Title: SheBreathes Soul Stories

Description: 1st Edition, Boston, MA

Subject: Self-Actualization, Spiritual, Growth and Healing

Edited by Beth Knaus

Manufactured in the United States of America

Book Design by Robin Pawlak-Garstka

Author Photos by Robin Ganter

DEDICATION

For the incredible women whose stories illuminate these pages, this collection is a heartfelt tribute to you and to all the remarkable women who have faced challenges head-on, shown incredible strength, and shared their unique journeys.

To the mothers, daughters, sisters, and friends who have pushed boundaries and paved the way for others - this is dedicated to you.

TABLE OF CONTENTS

INTRODUCTION

I published my first book, *Embody Your Essence: Breaking Patterns of Suffering and Reclaim Your Joy*, within one month of my 60th birthday. I had embarked on what I called my "jennassaince," which centered around my intention to direct 100% of my energy into heart-centered initiatives that spark joy within me.

My inspiration for writing *Embody Your Essence* came from deep contemplation regarding my own life and a desire to develop more conscious connections with the people in my life. After nearly six decades in this energy body, I had realized the heart of the matter: when we open ourselves up, show our vulnerability, and share our real stories, we not only begin to heal ourselves, but we heal one another.

I feel compelled to serve as a catalyst for a movement toward people being more consciously connected — to a safe space where we find the courage to show up with empathy, authenticity, a recognition of shared values and common experiences, and a safe, supportive container in which to share who we really are at our deepest layers.

In a world where most of us are hiding to stay "safe,"
speaking our vulnerable truth may be one of the most
courageous things we can do.

So I chose courage. I dug deep. I owned my story. I published my book.

I began standing up and speaking out to everyone who would listen to the stories I was sharing about my own healing journey. I talked very openly, for the first time, about my darkest moments and how I had kept them hidden for so long because, like most people, I lived in fear of being misjudged and of not belonging.

There were moments when I fell back into old limiting belief patterns and felt my inner child desperately seeking acceptance, acknowledgement, and validation from others relating to my book. When I wasn't getting the response I had hoped for from the people I craved it from most, I began regretting my decision to expose myself so completely in this way, and that led to some sleepless nights.

And then a remarkable thing happened.

Perfect strangers began reaching out to me through social media to thank me for writing the book. Women began sharing how my story mirrored events in their own lives. Readers expressed how my courage to be vulnerable had inspired them to open up about their own painful life experiences and move beyond their fear and limiting beliefs. It was validating to learn that my work had hit home for my target audience of women on a path of re-awakening.

I remembered that the only validation I really needed regarding my work was my own. We all know that healing is an ongoing process; it's not a one and done experience. So as I worked my way through the process of becoming, I felt another enormous release. Release of expectations. Release of shame. Release of those lingering limiting beliefs and feelings of unworthiness. I remembered that we are here to understand ourselves, not to be understood by others, and I regained the confidence to share my story.

It was in those moments that I was divinely inspired to create another book. I knew there was a "Shequel" on the way and that, this time, it would be a collection of stories from women who had moved through life's challenges with both grit and grace. I began encouraging members in my circle to join me on this truth-telling adventure. The concept for the SheBreathes Soul Stories collection was born.

I had created the SheBreathes Balance Women's Collaborative in 2016 as a platform for empowerment, education, and advocacy of women on the rise to connect and collaborate personally and professionally. All these years later, I knew we had the strength of community to co-create this compelling collection of soul stories to inspire growth and healing. As anticipated, one by one, these 22 brave women stepped forward, moving beyond their own limiting beliefs and choosing courage over fear.

Every one of us has journeyed through this life, carrying with us tales of love, loss, triumph, and transformation. This collection of stories is a treasury of narratives that celebrates the resilience, wisdom and spirit of women everywhere. Within these pages lie the threads that connect us all — love, betrayal, heartbreak, self-discovery, and personal growth.

In this anthology, we explore the depths of the divine feminine, illuminating the intricate balance between strength and vulnerability. Each story unfolds so beautifully, revealing the layers of a woman's life — her hidden struggles, the glimmers of growth, her leaps of faith, and the moments that shaped her journey and had everything to do with who she is today. We touch upon themes of addiction, trauma, sexual abuse, illness, grief and loss, love, discrimination, and self-realization. These stories invite reflection and empathy, as we are reminded of the strength and power that comes from our own self compassion, authenticity, and resilience.

The SheBreathes Soul Stories Collection is an invitation to embrace the depth of our shared humanity. As you turn each page, you'll encounter the power of shared experiences, discovering that, regardless of our backgrounds, we are united by the common thread of womanhood. Our stories serve as a reminder that every woman's truth is a vital piece of the larger human narrative, and when shared, it has the potential to create waves of change and understanding.

It is a celebration of the countless voices that deserve to be heard, cherished, and celebrated. Whether you are seeking inspiration, connection, or simply an opportunity to listen and learn, this anthology is a powerful testament to the resilience and strength found in the hearts of women. Open your heart and mind to their truth telling and prepare to be forever changed by the experience.

Much Love & Light,

Jennifer

Jennifer

JENNIFER SULLIVAN

GROWING UP WITH SPIRIT: THE GHOST OF MARY ANN ELY

Hey Mom, guess what? I talk to dead people!

This isn't exactly how I announced it, but for those who meet me now, it's one of the ways I introduce myself. Hello, my name is Jennifer Sullivan, and I am a psychic, rescue medium, astrologer, and firewalk facilitator. I'm sure you are smiling and nodding, wondering what the hell any of that means, and part of you might even be questioning my sanity. This is why I kept my gifts on a "need-to-know" basis for most of my life, due to fear of judgment from my friends, family, and society.

I was adopted when I was 18 months old, by Bobbie and David Sullivan. Anyone who has had a child knows the chaos in preparing for one, especially the first — the painstaking effort and attention to detail like choosing paint colors, decorations, toys, and safety measures throughout the home. My parents didn't have that experience — they had a whirlwind twenty-four hours. My mom met me and spent time with me in the townhouse in Boston, along with my foster mother and the social worker from Catholic Charities. After that one hour, my mom had to decide: Yes or No. Surprise! She said yes and went home to prepare their new, fixer-upper Victorian home in Scituate, Massachusetts for a walking, talking, sassy-mouthed toddler to arrive the very next afternoon!

Spoiler alert: this child also could see and talk to dead people!

My mother will say I was a great sleeper, and I was the first one up in the morning. She would wake up to me carrying on, laughing, and having one-sided conversations with "myself." When she opened the door to my bedroom, I clearly was busy. She will say she was not aware of having any supernatural experiences in that house. My dad would say he always knew there was someone else there. Friends of mine, as well as house sitters, had experiences. Some were freaked out, while others thought it was super cool.

So, who was I talking to? I grew up with Mary Ann Ely, the matriarch of the Ely family, the original builders of the home. Mary Ann adored that home and was often seen in my parent's room, the main bedroom of the house with an incredible ocean view.

Webster's Dictionary defines a medium as "an individual held to be a channel of communication between the earthly world and a world of spirits." Seems simple enough. Almost everyone has been exposed to mediumship in some form — in person, in books, or in film and television. There are a few assumptions that come with mediumship, like being able to see and talk to all dead people, that it can happen at any time, and that perhaps, those of us who do see and talk to dead people might be slightly unhinged. When I tell others that "I talk to dead people," there is either disbelief, fascination followed by questions, or utter horror.

Oh, and there was one time when I mentioned it, and the people I was with immediately started praying for my soul. That made for a super uncomfortable moment.

In the mediumship community, there is a divide. Some will swear that souls cannot get "stuck" and that all souls naturally cross over. And then there are those who believe that not all souls cross — they end up sticking around. I fall into this category; however, I respect others who have different views. My personal experience, along with mentors and research, leads me to believe the following: souls can remain earthbound due to trauma, confusion, or unfinished business with loved ones, or perhaps their souls must experience something before they can leave. Some of these souls may have a contract with someone living, something they need to fulfill before being able to cross.

I often wonder if there are contracts between the living and the dead, and if this is why Mary Ann Ely and I connected. It makes sense on some cosmic level if we had a soul contract that we both had to fulfill before she could cross. If so, what was that contract? Guarding that house she built and loved so much, and more importantly, teaching me, the overly independent, sassy-mouth girl with a Sagittarius Stellium, how to communicate with spirits.

Hats off to Mary Ann — that was no easy task!

Flashback to me being a happy, opinionated toddler, doing

mostly normal toddler things with my mom and dad. But I knew there was someone else in that house. A lady in a blue dress, with a high collar, buttons, black boots with small, chunky heels that laced up, and her hair in a tight bun. She had a stern but gentle presence and was like another parent. But I was the only one who could see her. I was confused and couldn't understand why my parents couldn't see her, too. She sat at the dining room table when we ate dinner, walked the halls at night, checked in on me when I went to bed, and was the first person I talked to in the morning when I woke up. I was never afraid of this woman, who told me her name was Mary Ann. She would play with me, follow me around the yard, and scold me when I wandered too far. Sometimes I found her annoying.

After all, what child wants to always listen to their parents? And then have a weird third parent that's a ghost also telling them what to do?

I had a distinct memory as a child of playing with some toys, and my mom coming in and asking what I was doing.

I shrugged and said, "Playing with Mary Ann." I'm sure she thought it was the name of a stuffed animal, doll, or an imaginary friend. If I had said, "I'm playing with the ghost that lives here that you can't see," then I'm sure my mom would've had a different reaction.

There came a point when I asked Mary Ann why people couldn't see her. She was blunt with her answers, never mincing words, and told me she knew that she was dead, that she was a ghost, and that she chose to stay here. She made it clear that the house was her house; she just allowed people to live in it. She told me that she knew she could leave, but she had "something to take care of." She refused to elaborate on the subject, and I didn't push it, since I had learned through other interactions that she only gave information that she deemed necessary.

I started seeing more spirits out in public. There was a lovely old lady spirit I talked to at the grocery store while my mom waited in line. When my mom came to collect me, she would ask who I was talking to, and I would roll my eyes and say, "The same lady I talk to every week." She gave me some strange looks, but never pushed the issue. I'm sure she was just happy to be out of the store, wanting to quickly load up the minivan, and get home. But I had questions. Who were these people? Why did they often have "old-timey" clothing? Why couldn't everyone see them? Do they choose to stay here like Mary Ann? I would talk to Mary Ann about the spirits I saw and the conversations I had. The only earthbound spirits I had encountered so far were friendly and mostly seemed elderly, because a little kid thinks everyone is ancient.

Then one night, I had an encounter with a not-so-nice being in my house when I was around seven or eight. There was a shadowy figure in my room, and for the first time in my life, I was terrified. I knew whatever this thing was didn't feel "safe," and I hid under my covers like a kid in some horror movie, shaking, my eyes glued shut, trying to make sure it couldn't see me. Mary Ann hadn't shown up, which was strange. I wonder if there had been some kind of block preventing her from being in the room at that time. This spirit, entity, or whatever the hell it was, messed with me, and I started screaming bloody murder. My parents came running, whipping the door open. Whatever that thing was darted out and into the hallway, and Mary Ann was pissed and on a mission. I cried, saying I was frightened, and my parents got me settled after some time. I told them to remove the night light because I associated the light with the shadowy figure. My parents did this without question, and eventually went back to bed, leaving the door open so they could hear me if anything else happened.

After they went to bed, Mary Ann appeared and sat with me. She told me she would make sure nothing like that ever came into the house again. She offered to stay in my room, and I agreed. She also told me to remove the mirror from my dresser. The following morning, I told my parents I didn't want a mirror in my room anymore, and Dad dug out the tools and removed it. The bedroom set was my mother's from her childhood, and that mirror was a silver-backed mirror, which I didn't realize at the time. I didn't learn until high school that mirrors, particularly silver-backed ones, can be portals. To this day I do not sleep with a mirror in my room, and when I travel, I bring materials that are enchanted with protection to cover mirrors in my hotel rooms. I also perform a ritual to seal the mirrors, closing any portals that shouldn't be open.

I see and interact with enough spirits without having other open portals, thank you.

Mary Ann honored her word. I've had some wild experiences with spirits in other places, but Mary Ann made damn sure that I never had to experience that ever again. She never allowed anything into that house in Scituate that did not meet her approval.

When I was 11 years old, I discovered tarot, instantly falling in love. It's still my favorite form of divination today. I met some other girls into "witchy stuff" when I was in high school and found my first living mentor, a petite five-foot-tall, red-haired witch who owned a metaphysical shop in Weymouth called The Middle Earth South. Sandy happily took me under her wing, and I met with her as often as possible. She helped me develop a way to turn my ability "off" when needed. At that point, I would just choose not to engage with spirits if I didn't want to, but if they were persistent, I didn't know what to do, and I didn't want to ever piss one off since I had no clue how to handle that.

I felt empowered by Sandy's teachings, and I read any book on witchcraft I could get my hands on and did tarot spreads daily. I would talk to Mary Ann about all this, and she just listened. I was fortunate that she was not judgmental about it, and that even though I had been raised as a Catholic, my parents were super chill about their daughter being into all that "stuff." My dad even took me shopping at occult stores, which were few and far between at the time.

Mary Ann might not have been judgmental about the witchy stuff going on; however, she was when it came to potential boyfriends or actual boyfriends. I had a friend come over the house, who I'll call Ron, whom I really "liked" at the time. Remember, the house was a huge Victorian with around fifteen rooms. The main staircase was ornate and covered by an Oriental-looking carpet. This would've been the staircase reserved for family use only. There was another staircase, directly attached to the kitchen, which had been used by staff, servants, etc. That day, Ron came to the house for the first time and went up that main staircase. We hung out, watched a movie or something, and eventually, he went to leave. I could sense Mary Ann watching the whole time, and Ron even saying "I feel like I'm being watched" a couple of times, which I playfully shrugged off, saying he just wasn't used to being in an old house. When it came time to leave, I walked down the stairs to show him out, and all of a sudden he went tumbling down, nearly taking me out in the process.

I immediately freaked, like any normal teen, and shouted, "Oh my God — are you okay?!"

Ron looked at me, shaking, and said, "Something just pushed me down the fucking stairs!"

I looked up, and Mary Ann was at the top of the stairs, her arms folded, wearing a displeased expression. I was pissed and tempted to flip her off and start cursing her out.

The jig was up — I told Ron there was a ghost in the house, her name was Mary Ann, and that clearly, she was an asshole. He was very cool about it, which of course, impressed me (remember I'm sixteen here), and picked himself up and cracked some jokes. After he left, I had a long talk with Mary Ann about not interfering with my dating life and that she couldn't push boys down the stairs that she didn't like. She was less than amused and reminded me that it was her house, and being the smartass I am, I reminded her that she was dead and explained that dating is different in these times. She reluctantly agreed not to push men down the stairs anymore. Ron and I dated off and on for a few years. Each time he came over, he would look at me, and ask, "Is it cool with the ghost if I go upstairs?" And he often used the stairs located in the kitchen, rather than the main staircase, out of fear, respect, or both.

So, nothing more than chaste kissing ever occurred in that house or on that property with anyone I dated. Nothing will kill the mood quicker than a Victorian-era ghost staring at you, shaking her head while you are trying to make out.

Mary Ann reneged on the "no pushing men down the stairs" agreement only once. Years later, my friend Kerry came to live with me for a short time after my dad passed, while my mom was away for a few months for an artist in residency program. Kerry's boyfriend came to visit, and he got shoved down the stairs. Kerry knew about Mary Ann, since we had been friends since high school and got along with her just fine. But Mary Ann clearly did not like the boyfriend. We knew it was Mary Ann, because he mentioned that he "felt like someone pushed him." Thankfully, he wasn't hurt, and she didn't repeat the process, although he was extremely careful when walking down the stairs after that. Kerry isn't with this person anymore, and we laugh about the incident occasionally when we talk. Kerry always says, "See, Mary Ann knew what was up – I should've dumped him right then. Mary Ann was a good judge of character."

As strict and opinionated as Mary Ann was, she had a softness and kindness. As I stated before, she had this motherly vibration at times, which was greatly appreciated. One of the most powerful times I experienced this was the night my dad died.

David Sullivan could have an entire book written about him – and who knows, maybe someday I will write that. He was a very spiritual soul, and he died unexpectedly on Holy Thursday, April 13, 2006. It was fitting that David Sullivan passed on Holy Thursday, due to his connection with the Blessed Mother Mary. We received the news around 8:30 p.m. when a police officer came to the house to notify us. Immediately, we made phone calls to family. His best friend, Timmy, immediately drove down to the house in disbelief, realizing it was true when he saw me sitting on the porch steps sobbing, and he offered to stay the night. My mother and I were in shock, and after the whirlwind, we eventually tried to go to bed, while Timmy stayed downstairs on the couch.

I knew I wasn't going to be able to sleep that night. My mind was going a million miles an hour, my Virgo Moon brain going over every possible scenario about how things would change for my mom and me. I was so overwhelmed, and I wondered if it was physically possible for your body to run out of tears to cry. I was lying on my side, quietly weeping into my pillow. I heard the door open and footsteps enter the room. I ignored this and remained on my side, too sad, too tired, too overwhelmed to acknowledge whoever it was. I felt the bed shift, someone sitting on the edge, inching their way up to me, a thigh just barely touching my back. I continued to cry, a new wave of "what ifs" playing out in my head, refusing to turn around. And then, a hand was on my shoulder, and I thought it was my mother. A new flood of tears fell as I buried my face in my pillow and wailed. The touch that came from that hand was full of love, tenderness, and compassion that I hadn't ever experienced before. There were no words — just gentle caresses.

I couldn't tell you how long that went on for — but it was a while. Finally, I stopped crying. The hand stilled, returning to my shoulder, offering a slight reassuring squeeze, and then the hand was gone. The weight from the bed lifted, and I finally turned around to thank my mom for sitting with me like that. I shifted, feeling the hand fall away, and when I rolled, expecting to see my mom, there was Mary Ann, now standing by the door, looking towards my parents' bedroom at the opposite end.

I was stupefied, having about the hundredth "what the fuck" moment that night, and not having the mental or emotional compacity to thank her for what she had just done. She didn't say anything, but instead looked at me, then opened the door and stepped into the hall. For whatever reason, I was compelled to get out of bed, and without turning the light on, I went to the doorway. At the same time, my mother's door creaked its way open, and suddenly I was staring at her in the doorway to her bedroom. I remember my mom being confused, trying to focus her vision on me at the end of the hall. Without hesitation, I made my way down the hall to my mom.

"I can't sleep," she muttered, completely drained. "It's a little weird that the door just opened, and you were standing in your doorway."

"It's been a really weird night," I replied. I honestly didn't know what else to say.

My mom stepped back, and I followed her into the bedroom. Mary Ann wasn't hanging around, giving us privacy. I climbed in next to my mom, in the spot my dad had slept for so many years, wondering if I had completely lost my mind. The two of us stayed up, talking about Dad, the wake and funeral, and what we were going to do going forward. The sun eventually rose, and we both mustered the courage and energy to face the day, knowing it would be challenging but taking comfort in having each other.

I'll never forget that night and will be infinitely grateful to Mary Ann for showing so much compassion. She knew my mom and I needed each other, even though the two of us couldn't see it at the time. I didn't tell my mom right away about what happened, but when I did, she was stunned into silence, sitting quietly for a while, taking time to process. Occasionally, she brings it up, and we talk about it, and usually says something like, "Yeah, that thing with the doors opening and us seeing each other was so weird," and we usually get a good chuckle out of it.

Years later, we decided to put the house on the market, and I wondered what would happen when we left. My mom told the realtor that I had interactions with a ghost in the house, and he asked my mom if she had any experiences. She said no, because she honestly felt like she didn't, and therefore the realtor didn't feel the need to disclose the information. I had conversations with Mary Ann about us leaving, and feeling sad about not having her around. She had been such a huge part of my life, and going to live in a place with no ghost was going to be a whole new experience for me.

Mary Ann told me we had been "excellent caretakers" of the Scituate home, and she appreciated the work my parents had done over the years. We had been very selective whenever updates were done, making sure the "feel" of the home was never lost. Everything was up to date, but you knew it was an old house when you entered, from the crown molding, high ceilings, built-in bookcases, and picture windows overlooking the ocean. Mary Ann was big on having the integrity of the house maintained — and there would've been hell to pay if my parents hadn't been so innately and intuitively connected to keeping the spirit of that house alive.

I asked Mary Ann if she would stick around, or if she was finally ready to leave. At this point, I had learned about crossing spirits over and had some experience with that. I had offered to assist if she was willing to go, and I recall her shrugging and saying she hadn't decided what she was going to do yet. I rolled my eyes and told her not to go stirring up trouble with the new owners, and not to torment the people who were building on the property below, since the view from the picture window in the bedroom would be partially blocked by the new home. She wasn't pleased with the building but knew we had tried to fight it for years and lost the battle.

My last night in that house, I remember being up late, and the lights flickering as they often did. This had always been Mary Ann's signature way of telling me it was late and to go to bed. She would do this at midnight, and there were many times when I had to explain that I was writing papers for college and cursed her out when she turned the lights off. Mary Ann, the eternal mother figure, telling her kid to get their ass in bed. I remember laughing that final night and choosing to listen to her.

I finished up some last-minute packing and then climbed into bed. The following morning, I asked her once more if she was ready to cross over and if she wanted my help. She smiled kindly and declined, saying she still hadn't made up her mind, and that she would go when she was ready.

Mary Ann was always an opinionated woman, both in life and as a spirit.

I remember driving to the house to go to the beach a few months after moving and tapping into the energy of the property, scanning for Mary Ann to see if she was still there. I waited patiently, seeing if she would show, but was pleased when I couldn't trace her signature. Although there was something sad about not feeling or seeing her, I was so happy that she had found peace. She had fulfilled that thing she "needed to do" before crossing over that she had mentioned so many times and had finally made the decision to cross over.

I share stories about Mary Ann a lot, as she was such a key figure in my life. My mom and I talk about her, and friends both new and old, get to hear about her. Most people talk about the lives of the living that have impacted them, and here I am talking about a dead woman from the 1800s who was my teacher, friend, mentor, and parental figure.

It's funny how Spirit works. I sometimes wonder if I hadn't had Mary Ann in my life, how my mediumship skills would've developed. She showed me that spirits aren't something to be feared, but something to be respected, and that they can be lost, just like us. And for those souls that are earthbound deserve compassion just like the living. Because let's face it, if the world had more compassion in it, it would be a very different place.

So, thank you, Mary Ann Ely, for sticking around in Scituate, Massachusetts until I came along. Whether it was due to a soul contract between us, or just because you loved that house and wanted to continue seeing that incredible view of the waves crashing from the main bedroom — my heart is filled with gratitude for the knowledge imparted to me.

My heart is full.

Jennifer Sullivan discovered her ability to communicate with earthbound spirits at a young age. Later she further developed her psychic skills, learned Tarot, and now does readings professionally. She began studying astrology, falling in love with the planets and stars, and unique patterns within everyone's chart. She offers astrology readings to clients so they can better know themselves and their loved ones, and what's going on energetically around them.

Additionally, Jennifer is a firewalk facilitator. Firewalking gives you an opportunity to heal, connect to the ancient element, and create bonds with those who experience it with you.

She is also a practicing Witch, Psychic Medium, and holds certifications in Usui Reiki as a Master/Teacher, Akashic Records, Selenite & Sound Facilitation, Sundoor Firewalk & Glasswalk Instruction.

Jennifer offers private readings one-on-one, with families, or groups. She also designs crystal jewelry and spiritual tools to be incorporated into your daily life and your spiritual practice.

Learn more about Jennifer at: www.jennifer-sullivan.com

Danielle

DANIELLE CLEARY

THE POWER OF HEALING WITH INTENTION

Spring 2017: what I now jokingly refer to as The Spring of Our Discontent. Perspective allows me to laugh and wonder at the depths of horror we were facing; at the time, we were not fully aware of what lay ahead. On paper, we should have been thriving. The spring of 2016, I completed a health coach certification program, finally claiming a career path that I pursued in my spare time for many years. I launched a business soon after, Compass Coaching & Wellness, and started seeing clients. My husband Jerry and I had been together for 18 years and still enjoyed each other's company, still finding ways to dance, laugh, and play. We were raising two kind, happy sons, and had great family support.

Then the crisis came, after brewing since early 2016, when my elder son Dylan started having some strange strep infections. Severe stomach pains that kept him up all night and forced him to miss three days of school yielded a diagnosis of strep throat and an ear infection. Weird, but we treated him with antibiotics and got back to business. September 2016 brought another strange infection, a cellulitis reaction to a routine vaccine at his physical. Our family doctor assured me he had never seen that in all his years of practice. We found ourselves back at the urgent care over Labor Day weekend and Dylan's 10th birthday. Three days later, Dylan started fourth grade on a cocktail of antibiotics and steroids.

Midway through September I celebrated my 40th birthday with Jerry in the woods, a welcome retreat from the pressures I felt building. I felt drained by the demands of life. Energetically, I felt off, and I wasn't sure of the source. Was it the added responsibility of launching my own health coaching business? Was it juggling children, marriage, household, and work while also trying to reclaim a bit of who I was before all of that? Or was something else at play?

By October, I had stopped enrolling new clients in my health coaching programs and had determined I needed to return to work outside of the home, where the boundaries would be more clear. By November, Dylan entered a full-blown mental health crisis, experiencing an overnight onset of OCD and anxiety, with no clear trigger.

It started the Friday after Thanksgiving, after being at the movies. We walked in the door, and Dylan paused in the downstairs hallway, stripped down to his underwear, and asked me to wash everything he had been wearing, including his jacket, hat, and gloves. He sprinted upstairs to the shower. From that point forward, Dylan showered EVERY SINGLE NIGHT before getting into his bed. If I denied him a shower for any reason, it created serious distress for him. As a mom to two boys, I've heard plenty of tales of young men with no interest in personal hygiene. This obsession with cleanliness, accompanied by extreme emotional reactivity, concerned me deeply.

Shortly after Thanksgiving, I joined a gym and booked an appointment with a therapist, desperate to stay ahead of the stress that was bearing down on me. I published a blog post on December 15, 2016 entitled "Going Dark", alluding to the struggles we were all facing. A crisis for one of us meant a crisis for all of us, as we are too intertwined for it to be any other way. As our family closed out that year that had held so much promise and so much hope, I retreated inward and braced myself for the months ahead.

Those late winter/early spring months of 2017 passed in a blur. In January, I locked down a job facilitating a Diabetes Prevention Program through the YMCA and had a clear checkup with my gynecologist, where she recommended a screening mammogram, as I had just turned 40. In February, we met with a neuropsychiatrist, who diagnosed Dylan with generalized anxiety and obsessive-compulsive disorder (OCD) tendencies. We discussed doing some testing, but the specialist recommended we start Dylan on Cognitive Behavioral Therapy (CBT) first, and we could discuss further evaluations with whichever doctor we connected with. I was eager for him to start treatment. Dylan's emotions were all over the map, and school was becoming a challenge, both academically and socially. Although he had been on an IEP (Individualized Education Program) for both reading and writing in his early elementary years, he had made tremendous progress with the support of Jerry and myself, his teachers, and his specialists. Dylan was now reading above his fourth-grade level and had completed his

IEP for writing in the spring of 2016, at the end of third grade. His teacher at that time had found it difficult to believe that writing was ever a struggle for him.

In the fall of 2016, he earned his best report card of elementary school, and it felt like Dylan was really coming into his own academically. That all changed in early 2017. Dylan was having a hard time keeping up with classwork. His handwriting was deteriorating. His emotional responses to situations seemed extreme and inappropriate. Was this the onset of puberty? I thought maybe it was the increasing academic demands as the school year progressed — he's always had a wonky, grip and the physical act of writing doesn't come easily for him.

By March 2017, Dylan was back in weekly occupational therapy (OT) to practice keyboarding, since handwriting was so difficult for him. In late March, we added weekly CBT appointments, and I desperately hoped that we would start seeing improvements. It felt like my bright and capable child was spiraling into mental illness and I couldn't pull him back no matter how hard I tried. I knew that what we were seeing was anxiety and OCD, but I kept telling Jerry that I felt like we were missing something. I felt like there was something at the source of all of this we hadn't yet identified. March is also the month that I first felt a small hard spot in my right breast. I attributed it to muscular changes from three months of strength training, and booked a screening mammogram for the earliest availability, in late May. I then turned my attention back to my child, who seemed to be worsening, despite our best efforts.

Dylan held it together every day at school; when he returned home, he was a wreck. I dreaded the five hours from bus dropoff to bedtime. At our IEP meeting in early April, Dylan's teacher asked me to be his scribe at home so that we could save him the frustration of writing but still get his thoughts on paper. I found myself sitting beside my fourth grader night after night, reminding him to focus, calming him down, and writing for him as needed. I tried different strategies for our homework sessions, without success. By late April, Dylan started to have "episodes" — they seemed like what might be panic attacks. Something would cause him to feel frustrated or upset, and he couldn't let it go. His fits grew in intensity, and by early May he was hitting himself in the face as his anger with himself increased. At a loss for how to help, I just held him, hugged him, and cried with him. It was clear I was losing my child, but to what, I did not know.

On May 7, 2017, I opened an article a friend had shared several weeks earlier, entitled "Mom Thought Child Had Mood Swings, Not a Neurological Disorder." The article talked about PANDAS (Pediatric Autoimmune Neuropsychiatric Disorders Associated with Streptococcal Infections) and the five criteria that help doctors diagnose it: "Significant obsessive/compulsive behavior or tics, abrupt onset of symptoms, a patient of prepubescent age, a history of strep infection, and a mix of other neurological symptoms such as loss of appetite, bed-wetting, decreased school performance and behavioral regression." I searched online for as much information as I could about PANDAS and learned that our family history of rheumatic fever and mental illness increased our risk for this condition. Both rheumatic fever and PANDAS are autoimmune illnesses; the body produces strep antibodies to fight the infection, and those antibodies end up attacking healthy tissue instead. My mother had undiagnosed rheumatic fever as a child; her heart was so damaged that she experienced a stroke and required open heart surgery by the time she was 34 years old. In Dylan's body, the strep antibodies were attacking his brain; unchecked, who knew where that would lead?

The next week, I met with Dylan's doctor and took him for bloodwork. His strep antibodies were higher than the normal range, so they started him on antibiotics. Jerry and I took a much-needed vacation to Mexico, where we celebrated a friend's wedding. We returned home on May 23rd, just before bedtime, and Dylan asked, "I don't need to take a shower tonight, do I?" I started crying. My boy had been obsessively showering every single night since November 25th. I gratefully assured him that it was fine to skip a shower that night. For the first time in months, I felt like we were moving in the right direction. The mystery illness that had defined our lives for the past six months was loosening its grip on my child.

Three days later, the Friday before Memorial Day weekend, I had my mammogram, where I mentioned the lump I had felt in early March. By this point, it had grown significantly. Cancerous tumors have an energy to them. They grow and metastasize by hijacking blood vessels to feed the cancer cells with oxygen and nutrients. At one point in the spring, I felt my heart ache for what my child was going through. I later realized that was the feeling of a tumor growing. Looking back, I probably should have moved the mammogram up. But I spent most of my adult life engaging in healthy practices that are supposed to prevent cancer, and I had a child who was in crisis. Subconsciously, I couldn't imagine a situation that I wasn't able to rebound from.

The mammogram led to an ultrasound, which led to a biopsy, which led to my cancer diagnosis day, June 13, 2017. It's a day I now celebrate (we celebrate ALL the wins!). That year, it was a day filled with overwhelm, shock, and fear.

I was diagnosed through my local hospital but chose to bring my case to Dana Farber Cancer Institute in Boston. My first appointment in DFCI was scheduled for June 21, 2017, the summer solstice. When facing an aggressive cancer diagnosis, eight days can feel terrifying. We live in a culture of fear around cancer, and we don't trust our bodies to heal themselves. I could feel people's fear for me. I could hear it in their voices on the phone, see it in their faces when we spoke in person, and read it in their text messages. I too started my healing journey filled with fear. I also felt a bit blindsided by the Universe. How could I be facing breast cancer? How did my body not fight this successfully? I had spent years cultivating a deep trust in the wisdom of my body. I had spent years giving my body what I thought it needed to be healthy and to heal. If my body allowed a cancerous tumor to grow, I chose to trust that it knew exactly what it was doing, and that tumor was the access to a higher version of health for myself moving forward. The body will do whatever it needs to keep us safe and protect us. That must mean that my body needed to create this tumor to protect me from something I wasn't able to see.

From June 13th forward, my mission was to rid my body of cancer. I went into action the moment I was diagnosed, a full 29 days before my first chemotherapy treatment. For my purposes, it didn't matter what kind of cancer cells were in my body, how far they had gone, or how fast-growing they were. What mattered was that I evict them from my body by any and all means at my disposal. For those four weeks, I used reiki, acupuncture, massage, cannabis, supplements, an alkaline diet, and the power of intention. Although I had already done some tests, the specialists at Dana Farber like to double-check things. For those four weeks, they sent me for biopsies, ordered scans, and analyzed tissue samples. As the results came back, many of them different than what I had originally received, my mission remained the same: kick cancer out of my body. Early July brought the news that there were two tumors, not one; that they were not grade II cancer cells, but grade III — the fastest growing type of cancer cells. They were strictly HER2+ cells, not also ER+ (straight HER2+ is a more aggressive type of cell); and the cancer had spread to at least one lymph node, despite no physical indication of that in my clinical exams.

These had the potential to be very dark days. Some of them were harder than others, especially for those around me who didn't inhabit my body and couldn't feel or know what I did. The darkest day for me was June 23rd, the last day of school for my children, the day I told them I had been diagnosed with cancer. I physically felt terrible, which was unusual for me — throughout the cancer experience, I normally felt pretty good. Maybe finally acknowledging this illness in front of my kids made me feel unwell, or perhaps I could fully feel the weight of the journey ahead.

Having just met my doctors at Dana Farber on June 21st, I had not done the scans and biopsies that would reveal the true aggressiveness of the cancer I was facing. I didn't yet know the "facts" of my situation. Filled with fear, uncertainty, and physical pain as I lay in bed on the night of the 23rd, I knew I had a choice. I had to take control of the story that I was creating. On the darkest of days, I chose that this would be a story of healing.

In the months leading up to my diagnosis, I had felt the cancer in my body, and I felt the energy of the tumors growing. On Saturday, June 24th, the day after I consciously changed my story, I felt that energy lessen. In the space of fear and pain that I felt that Friday night, my brain wanted to think that I must feel so terrible because this is what it feels like when cancer is spreading. I knew that creating the future from that space was not going to go well. I asked Jerry to sit with me while I actively transformed the story from "This is what it feels like when cancer is spreading" to "This is what a body feels like when it's kicking cancer out." The next 24 hours brought about a healing crisis, triggered by the numerous healing modalities I pursued while waiting to start chemotherapy and cemented by the story I created about what was happening in my body. Hippocrates, the first person to coin the name cancer (he lived from 460-370 BC and called cancerous masses "karkinos," the Greek name for "crab"), also reportedly said, "Give me the power to produce fever, and I'll cure all disease."

On the afternoon of June 24, 2017, I ran a fever localized to my chest. I lay in bed for several hours, heat radiating from my torso, unable to focus on a book or movie or anything besides my fevered state. I experienced hallucinations during this experience I heard voices, whispering to me that this was a story of healing. When the fever broke, the tumors felt different, less dense. The energy of the tumors had dissipated. They no longer pulsed and throbbed and owned the landscape of my body. The mind-body connection is a powerful mechanism to behold.

The next two weeks were filled with medical appointments. I endured mammograms, ultrasounds, a bone scan, a CT scan, and an echocardiogram. On June 29th, Dana Farber biopsy day, I had 15 needles jammed into my breast; I learned that day that cancer bleeds because of all the blood vessels the tumor has hijacked to feed itself. The swelling and bruising from that procedure stayed with me for two and a half weeks. During that window of time, I couldn't feel what was happening with the tumors; when I started a clinical trial for chemotherapy on July 12th, my doctor still couldn't get an accurate measure. But I held fast to my story of healing, even as the results of the biopsies came back indicating that my breast cancer profile was as aggressive as they come.

On July 17th, five days after my first chemo treatment, the swelling from the biopsies finally went down, allowing me to feel what was going on in my chest. I did not feel any tumors. On August 2nd, I went for my second chemo treatment, and my oncologist confirmed that she also didn't feel any tumors, just some scar tissue. Regardless, we carried on with the plan, and I completed six rounds of a targeted chemotherapy clinical trial.

On November 17th, I underwent a lumpectomy, or breast conservation surgery. The surgeon removed four "sentinel nodes," which are the ones responsible to drain the cancer, along with the tissue that was marked as cancerous. For 11 days post-surgery, we waited. While we waited, I healed, my family carried all my heavy burdens, and we gathered with friends and family on our national holiday intended to give thanks.

On the evening of November 28th, 2017, I received a call from my surgeon — it was good news. The pathology was back on the tissue and lymph nodes they removed, and I had a "pathologic complete response," meaning there were no cancer cells left in the tissue that we knew was cancerous six months prior. We had our clean margins, and no further surgeries would be recommended at this time.

I know that the healing I initiated prior to the first chemotherapy infusion was instrumental in producing this outcome, and to this day I marvel at the power of our thoughts and intention to create our reality. I underwent another full year of treatment following the lumpectomy surgery and continued to use supplements and alternative or complementary therapies with great success. I didn't suffer as much as many cancer patients do, and I was able to minimize uncomfortable side effects from the more aggressive chemotherapy and radiation I received post-surgery. My son Dylan continued to heal as well. His healing has not always been linear; he's experienced backslides at times. But he's never revisited the depths of trauma that he endured for the six months prior to his diagnosis.

So much of healing from cancer or any major illness is a mental game. At the time of diagnosis, it wasn't helpful to dwell on how aggressive my particular cancer cells were. It was difficult to believe that I had cancer AT ALL; I chose to ignore that I had all the characteristics of a very aggressive cancer profile. I recognized early on in my own cancer journey that, as a cancer patient, I inherited a cultural conversation that had been passed down for thousands of years. For many of the patients who came before me, cancer did NOT go well. I can see now that in my early days of cancer diagnosis, it was just as important to fight off the cultural conversation as it was to heal from the physical cancer cells. I did not want to dwell on "what has happened to those before me." I chose to test the limits of what's possible. If I didn't know what was "expected" or "typical," then I could hang out in the land of possibility. It's there that I found my power.

I don't deny that there are very real physical conditions that sometimes cannot be overcome with the methods that I used. But when facing a health crisis, perhaps consider these questions: What stories are you telling yourself about your body? Is your body failing you, or is it protecting you? Is that pain caused by a worsening illness, or is that the pain of a healing crisis?

I don't say this to diminish the experience of those who have gone before me. I'm not here to judge their journey, only to share my own. I like to think that we all have a purpose in our lifetime, and sometimes that purpose is served in death; for others, it is served in life. Sometimes, the illness overwhelms the body, and it is time for the body to release the soul. And if that had been my path, I hope I would have chosen to travel it with power, strength, and dignity.

Danielle Cleary is an energy healer and health coach who loves to express herself through writing. Born and raised in Massachusetts, she earned her undergraduate degree in Romance Languages and Literature from Harvard University. Eager to escape the winters, she moved to San Diego after college and returned to New England after the birth of her first child.

Danielle started powerfully manifesting her future at a young age, declaring her intention to go to Harvard when she was just six years old. She loves to teach others how to use the power of intention in their own lives. Danielle feels most alive when exploring a new city or dancing to live music. She currently lives in North Attleboro, MA with her husband Jerry, two teenage boys, and a ridiculous muppet dog. She is grateful to her husband, family, and friends for their unwavering support and love.

You can follow Danielle on Instagram: @healthcoachcleary

Julie

JULIE GRIMM

BECOMING WHOLE

I had lived a life of adventure, travel, and love by the time I was 26. I grew up in an upper middle-class family, was well-educated, and had experienced many opportunities in life.

I traveled extensively to places like China, Israel, India, and a personal favorite, Paris. Returning to the States from Israel, I traveled through India solo and had an experience that altered the course of my life.

Up until that point, I had dove into new adventures freely and with little hesitation. I was involved with exploring my outside world and having adventures, learning, and studying. However, there were many parts of myself that I had not explored, and the real bravery I required in my life was diving into my inner world, and not the outer. For whatever reason – living on different continents and traveling alone was within my comfort zone – it didn't scare me. Other, less glamorous things – like examining my own behavior in relationships, or speaking up for myself, on the other hand, brought up terror.

At 26, I had a spiritual awakening, and it shook me out of my "normal" life and sent me on a journey to explore those inner worlds I had not yet gone to.

I say I had been living a "normal life" up until that point — which is true in so many ways, as I now see how many of us are living with our own demons, suffering daily, and unable to free ourselves from our pain — choosing instead to numb and ultimately avoid our true selves.

The truth was, I wasn't okay. As a child, I was sexually abused by someone close to me, and that unhealed trauma seeped into all aspects of my life: relationships, self-worth, money, and identity, to name a few. Most obvious and for clear reasons, it especially seeped into my sex life.

There were so many articles about how 20-30% of women couldn't orgasm from sex that I figured, that must just be me. There must just be something inherent in my wiring that blocks me from what is normal for others. Rather than more, I took this data point of anorgasmic women as a fact to resign myself to and didn't dig too much further.

I was programmed to look at sex from a purely physical and functional perspective. More than that, my generation boldly proclaimed, "I can have sex with whoever I like. Sleeping around is empowering!" I felt that having casual sex with people who didn't honor me was actually an expression of my liberation and freedom. I could devalue and ignore my own desires and emotions in the name of freedom! But in unconsciously acting from these programs and my own trauma, I avoided the deeper work of acknowledging what my true needs were and having to verbalize those to another person. In essence, I could hide from others, and most importantly, from myself.

A deeper consequence of the abuse was that an aspect of my mind had to always be in control. In order to feel safe, my mind had to keep a tight hold on my life, which kept me from dipping into dangerous emotions and feelings. I couldn't let go. I could build up a certain amount of my pleasure, but I couldn't allow myself to release it. Perhaps a part of me knew that if I did let go of control, those memories I was repressing and that enormous power within me would be free, and it would mean the destruction of all that had kept me safe those 26 years.

You see, I had no idea I was abused. That kind of abuse is shattering to a young soul and can be shattering to a whole family. In an instinctive act of self-preservation, I hid those memories deep within my psyche and repressed them so that I would forget until it was safe to remember — safe for that control valve within to release and exhale. It took me finally wanting to get close to someone and watching myself sabotage the relationship bit by bit, to realize that something was amiss within me.

Vital parts of myself were shut off in dark corners of my mind — fear, yes. Betrayal, yes. Hatred, yes. But also my access to my own pleasure, passion, power, and the goodness of life. So much had become inaccessible to me that I had been living a half-life, a partial expression of the truth of who I am, and was numb both to the pain as well as the joy.

After 20 or so years, the calling of my soul behind those walls grew so loud I had to answer. Not knowing what I was doing,

I began a quest for those very same memories I had buried long ago.

I followed the trail of my own inner puzzle until I found the walls of the Modern Mystery School. I started meditating regularly and felt that I could finally take a breath in the life that I had been drowning in. I did the Life Activation energy healing and started to remember my own creativity and joy. Finally, I attended the two-day Empower Thyself initiation, and something shifted within me. My own resistance to healing was now less than my desire to be whole. It took a significant amount of self-work and dedication to unlock those memories of abuse. From my understanding of childhood sexual abuse, there is the trauma of the actual abuse, but then there is an inherent denial that allows the abuse to perpetuate, and this denial, hardwired into family systems, is as corroding as the abuse. We say, "Believe in yourself." But what I found is that a key ingredient to believing in yourself is, quite simply, to believe yourself. At the core of my being, I had learned not to believe myself. Not to believe the feelings and emotions from my body, mind, and soul.

It was hard to admit the truth, which was repulsive to me. But that repulsion acted as an inner protective mechanism that also kept me separate from my own wholeness. Acceptance of reality, however I wished it were not true, allowed me to merge with the parts of myself gated behind my own disgust. I didn't have to protect myself or the people close to me from the truth any longer. I could welcome back the memories, and most importantly, all the aspects of myself I had banished. I could believe myself.

And in a moment, I became whole.

The gift I gave myself is inarticulable. On that day when I fully surrendered to my inner knowing, and when I finally chose to believe myself, colors became brighter. There was an immense peace that permeated all of life, and I felt that I'd reached some immense turning point, that I'd broken through a ceiling that had been limiting me my whole life. It was as if a puzzle piece had finally settled in, linking all of these seemingly strange and disconnected experiences and providing me with a deep understanding and compassion for myself.

Had I not found the Modern Mystery School and dedicated myself to healing, I would have lived and died never knowing or living the truth. Healing myself and choosing myself was never passive. It required my utmost dedication. My desire to heal and the power of my tools and support had to be greater than my desire to remain in ignorance.

Without the support of an ancient lineage, I would have seen the way my trauma poisoned my relationships, but never known why. I would have witnessed my numbness, but never truly known there was another side and never experienced living a life there. I can imagine myself, 70, 80 years old, reflecting on my life and seeing the outline my forgotten self made — but never knowing the cause. How could I have, when I didn't even know where to look?

This is the greatest gift I have given myself: to know myself, love, and accept myself. The tools I received through my training allowed me to create a safe haven within and trip the lock on memories 30+ years old, memories that were all but unreachable to me. More than that, it allowed me to update the operating system and coping skills I created as a traumatized five-year-old to present-day me — a capable, strong, and intelligent woman.

It is time for mankind to free itself from ancient fears and traumas, to rise into wholeness, and to embrace a new life.

I want to end this with something uplifting — to tell you it will all be OK. But that's not necessarily true. WE make it OK. Through our own efforts, we make it safe for our child selves — for our children. It's only through our work that anything changes — so yes, for me it will be OK, because I will make it OK, I am determined. We can all create that reality if we so choose. So tell me, will it be OK for you?

I don't know what monsters are guarding the trap doors of your minds, but I can guarantee you will be tested. Will you be brave enough to embark on your hero's quest and recover the treasure of your true self? That is up to each of us. The Modern Mystery School offers a path so that we do not lose our way — and many thousands have walked it throughout time to do just that. I hope that many thousands more will walk it, and that together we will shepherd into a new world. I hope that you find that courage within you, to conquer the fears that no one may ever see, that are not nearly as glamorous as exploring the world — that you find the bravery to explore your inner world and through that, embark on the greatest journey of all. A journey with the absolute greatest prize at the end — YOU.

May peace and light be with you all.

Julie Grimm always felt she was meant for more. She studied, and listened to teachers, mentors, and others, but somehow didn't feel like she was living her own life.

After a profound spiritual awakening in her 20s, she began seeking a path that would support her in living this life of more. She became an initiate in the ancient mysteries of life through the Modern Mystery School and began to discover that which was hidden in plain sight.

Julie had been undervaluing her gifts and didn't feel worthy of her big purpose. The tools of the Mystery School connected her with her true divine essence, and she reclaimed her light.

Now she helps others reclaim their light, power, and SOVER-EIGNTY so that they can give their gifts to humanity. If you feel the call to serve, to know yourself, please reach out to her. It would be Julie's honor to serve you.

You can learn more about Julie at: www.ohmbaby.com

Telma

TELMA SULLIVAN

MY JOURNEY THROUGH INFERTILITY AND ADOPTION

LIFE IS CREATED INSIDE US, WOMEN

After five years of being married, we decided to start trying to have a child. Nothing happened for months, so we sought our doctor's assistance. I was naive. I thought all it took to get pregnant was trying. I was in for a trip. We followed the physician's recommendations, which meant "timely trying." How fun is that?!

I remember thinking what an irony that some young women try so hard not to get pregnant and when they want to start a family, they find they can't conceive. That was me.

Timing is everything, but sometimes we need more than time. We reached out to a specialist, and we were put under the care of a fertility expert. A door opened into a world that seemed to provide magical solutions.

On our first visit to the clinic, while we were waiting to be seen, I saw a bunch of picture albums that included notes written by former clients. I picked one and started reading. They described the fertility journey and heartbreaks of women all over New England. I remember one particular letter where a woman underwent five in vitro fertilization cycles and miscarriages and was getting ready to try again. I was shocked, I couldn't imagine enduring five losses and being able to sign up for more. Once again, I had to face my misunderstanding that conception does not always happen, even when you are assisted by technology.

Infertility treatment is a multi-step process and not for the faint of heart. You plan, you schedule, you accept being "assisted," and you have to be able to relax in the hands of nurses, technicians, and doctors who are watching you, your partner, and your potential child or children.

After our initial lab work, the doctor suggested we try artificial insemination. Since I grew up spending my summers on a farm in Argentina where we used this method, I was very familiar with it, only that I never thought it would be used on me. The treatment room was sterile, without any pictures or furniture, and there was no music or anything else to hold my attention while I waited. I lay there, looking at the cold lights overhead, wishing I could talk to someone. The nurse entered, and after verifying my husband's and my identifying information, she proceeded to inseminate me. The emotions started escalating inside me. Was I going to get pregnant? Would I have a healthy child? What was the nurse's name again? Who was next door getting inseminated, too? How was I supposed to get pregnant in this non-nurturing environment? I took slow breaths to calm the racing thoughts. The nurse offered me a blanket. I was freezing and alone, having an out-of-body experience, one of the many I was about to deal with.

Waiting is never easy. This is not a death sentence, I said to myself. I did not have a cancer diagnosis, nor was I undergoing a life-threatening surgery. The treatments and procedures deprived me of excitement, I was anxiously and cautiously waiting for good news. There was no good news for a long while. Life could not be created inside my body. After three failed trials, we moved to the next level of fun, which needed more assistance.

LIFE CAN BE CREATED OUTSIDE US, WOMEN

We were recommended to try in vitro fertilization, the lady's letter and her five miscarriages still fresh in my mind. At this point, I had become more practical. The treatments had stripped all romanticism from the miracle of conception. Once I released that expectation, I regained a sense of excitement, and I felt this time things were going to work out.

The first in vitro attempt felt like the clinical team was attempting to get to know my body and how it responded to the drugs. I had to learn to do my own injections, a daily subcutaneous one in my belly and an intramuscular one in my butt at the end of each month. I practiced with an orange; I did what I had to do. The places where I injected myself remained sore years after, a physical memory of the journey. The medications changed my mood. I was tired, easily irritated, and sometimes I would cry for no apparent reason. My body was changing, too. I felt bloated and uncomfortable. The medical team normalized every symptom, "Your body is getting ready," they would often state. I traveled to do blood work at 7 a.m., then went to work and waited for the nurse's phone call around 4 p.m. to instruct me on the appropriate dosage. My work environment was an open space with no privacy. In the afternoons, I anxiously waited for the call, knowing that if I had any questions, my colleagues would be able to hear them.

I underwent my first retrieval where a few eggs were "force" fertilized in vitro. However, I was told they were "low quality" and not viable for transplant. Treatments were not consecutive. I had a sense of urgency but was required to take a month's break between treatments. At this point, my husband and I discussed how many trials we could afford emotionally. The failed results were starting to put a dent in my emotional state. I felt that my body was broken. It was not responding to the treatments. It was "behaving as an older body producing embryos of inferior quality," the doctor had mentioned. It was hard to accept those statements. I felt young and full of life and dreams. My husband's test results were normal. It was me who had the infertility issue.

I internalized the experience as if our challenge was my fault. He could have had children with someone else.

At that moment, I remembered something that my mother used to say. "When you graduate from college, I will adopt a little girl. There are so many children in the world that need a home." I would smile and never investigate the reasons for her statement. At that time, it didn't seem like it was something she would actually do. Often, we hear things that are somehow preparing us for the future.

On the second in vitro attempt, three "okay quality" embryos were transplanted. We had decided that it was our last treatment. On the day of the transfer, my husband was traveling overseas, so my father-in-law drove me to the clinic. It was the middle of the winter, and it was snowing. I remember being surrounded by the anesthesiologist, a couple of nurses, and the main doctor. He held my hand and started to count backward in Spanish until I fell asleep, "Diez, nueve, ocho." After three days of bed rest, I could get up and move. The doctor called and said, "We have good news, your blood work shows that you are pregnant. Congratulations!." I smiled. I had wanted to feel something growing inside me for so long. "Also, your hormones' high levels indicate that it's a double pregnancy. Two eggs have attached to your uterus." I was shocked. Not one but two, that felt amazing! Interestingly, twins run in my maternal family. "Keep doing what you are doing, we'll repeat the blood work in a few days. We have to take it one day at a time", he warned me. The impermanence of the news made me nervous, but it was the best news I had heard in a long while.

Wait and see is what I did until the next call. The nurse announced over the phone, "I am sorry, the pregnancy did not hold. The hormone levels dropped." You'll get your period." A flood of sadness entered my body. I was reminded again that my body had failed on our last attempt. I remembered the lady's letter once more and wondered if it was worth trying again. I wondered if that was what she did, try again, one more time, then one more time.

I was navigating with my heart, trying not to compare myself to other women's journeys into motherhood. Mine was my own.

That same weekend, I was invited to attend a baby shower. During the period I was doing fertility treatment, it seemed that everyone around me was having babies. I was not in the mood to attend any party, never mind a baby's arrival celebration. The mother-to-be was a friend who did not know my struggle. I felt guilty for not showing up, for not being able to support and celebrate her. My heart was broken, and I believed my body was too. I had purchased some baby outfits and toys to send to her. While I was wrapping them, I kept a onesie and a tiny white bear for my child, for the one, for the two I had lost. That night, I fell asleep sobbing, holding the bear close to my heart.

The next few weeks were hard, closing a chapter of a hundred pages. There was the emptiness of knowing that this other way of creating life was not available to us. It meant that we couldn't biologically have children and that I was responsible for leading my husband into a choice he would have not had to make if he was with another person. Day after day, I pondered this reality. I mourned the lost opportunities and tried hard to accept myself. This was a moment when I missed my mother, who had passed. I missed my father, who lived far away. I longed to be held by them like a child.

Fortunately, it was already spring, a season of renewed energy for me. Everything was blooming. I told myself it was time to rise and use my body for something else. I signed up to do a sprint triathlon. I started and ended my days swimming, biking, or running. My body was slowly releasing the leftover effects from the drugs and returning to its normal state. Sometimes you need to take a break from pushing toward a goal to vent, to grieve, to shed the weight, literally and figuratively. There was so much joy when I crossed that finish line. I had conquered something using my body. I was regaining my self-confidence and trust. There was another way to become a mother. I was not broken.

I wished I had asked my mother questions about her dream of adoption. I wished I knew more about her desire and motivations. In thinking about adoption, I reconnected with a thought I had had for a long time, even before being married or thinking about pregnancy. I had always felt that I didn't need to be pregnant to become a mother. I had never felt that the experience of being pregnant was important to me. What I wanted was to have children.

WE CAN EMBRACE A DIFFERENT LIFE, US, WOMEN

We started investigating adoption. Argentina, my country of origin, is not open to international adoptions, but it made sense to us to consider children from a Spanish-speaking country, to raise them bilingual and to have a connection with the language, for me. I went to an event and learned about adoption in Colombia and Ecuador. When the fall arrived, my husband was offered an international assignment in Romania. I was unsure of what the next chapter would look like. We accepted and departed.

The adoption journey was not easy or short. It felt like a pregnancy outside the body, presenting us with another set of questions to answer. We were evaluated by a psychologist to see if we were suitable potential parents. We were presented with a double-sided checklist page of medical conditions to see which ones we would accept. Would you accept a child with a heart condition? Would you accept a child with a cleft palate? Would you accept a child with a missing limb? Which age children would you accept? Would you consider siblings? They were two overwhelming, soul-searching pages.

We knew we wanted to have more than one child, and we were told that going through the adoption process more than once was difficult. It was mentioned that many sibling groups were never adopted since they are considered "hard to place." Most people want one child at a time.

We decided to apply for a sibling group under the age of four. This is the moment when you brace yourself, when you ask the universe to match you with whoever is meant to be in your life. Two months later, we were introduced by photos and documents to 18-month-old twins, a brother and sister. This is when you question yourself if you can embrace them and if they will do the same with you. We said yes, then we considered names. I started thinking about clothes and how long it would take to meet them. A few weeks went by, then we received a phone call. "Unfortunately due to a mistake, the twins were assigned to another couple who accepted them before you did." What?! My heart was bleeding. This felt like another miscarriage, only more real, more wrong. "There is nothing we can do," said the adoption representative. I felt like answering, "Don't worry, I've dealt with unexplainable outcomes before." I couldn't get the twins out of my mind. I wanted to know where they were going. I still remember them from the pictures. They are adults now, and I wonder how their life turned out. They could be my neighbors. The world is small.

Growth and comfort do not coexist. Growth always makes us uncomfortable; it takes us out of our comfort zone. I wasn't sure if I could keep trying. When you do hard stuff, it takes time and persistence. We took some time off to recharge and then returned to the search. Six months later, we were matched with eight-month-old twin girls. Twins again! I was anxious.

What if the process failed again? What if someone else took them? What if we weren't supposed to have children? I tried to imagine it, but I couldn't see myself without children.

We have a tendency to internalize failure, like something is wrong with us. I did that, but fortunately, I did not stop there. I've been a student of life, leading with an open mind, asking myself, "Why not?" Some days it's easier than others. When I work on the progress to get to the other side, I keep finding the doors.

My children are now grown. They are healthy, talented, kind, and beautiful. They are citizens of the world who are open to meeting new people with curiosity, just like they did when they met us. They are proud of who they are and where they've come from. I talk out loud with my mother and say, "Ma, I adopted twin girls, can you believe it?" Learning keeps expanding. My body is not a failure. It has given me the strength, courage, and the physical and mental abilities to embrace and love the two amazing individuals who I mother.

Telma Ferrari Sullivan is an independent Career Coach living with her family in the Greater Boston area. She is a native of Argentina and has lived in Bucharest, Romania, and Milan, Italy for several years. She enjoys reading, creative writing in Spanish, the arts, traveling the world, and the practice of yoga.

Telma can be contacted at: www.telmasullivan.com

Angela

ANGELA NUSS

CHILD-FREE AND MORE THAN OKAY THAT WAY

Growing up, I "always" thought I would get married by 30 and maybe have kids. Society told us that we were to get married, have a job, own a home, start a family, and maybe have a pet or two.

Not me.

I didn't have the same societal mindset as most women, but I didn't realize this until I was in college.

In the second half of my freshman year of college, my college friends and those from home started talking about the future, which happens to be one of my favorite topics. However, the more they talked about it, the more I felt less. Less what, you may be wondering?

Less emotion. Less desire. Less certainty.

I still didn't know what I wanted to do when I grew up. Yes,

I knew I wanted to help others and travel to Disney World many times. But that was the extent of it.

Then the topic of babies and kids started to come up in our conversations.

Nothing. I felt nothing.

Weird? Yes and no.

I was never entirely sold on the notion that everyone was meant to have children. Before you go jumping up and down and yelling at me for thinking that, I want to set the record straight about why children were not in my plan.

I think way too much. Obviously, my thoughts can go to extremes. I like to hope for the best and yet still be prepared for the worst. One of my careers actually depends on it.

I love people. I'm just not a diaper-changing, "raise kids for 18+ years" type of person.

I babysat some of my cousins and a neighbor when they were growing up. Was I the best babysitter? Heck no! Was I the worst babysitter? I would like to say heck no here as well. I just do better with kids who are potty trained, or at least a potty trainer in progress. I was only a kid myself — a teen, certainly not an adult — when I babysat for at least three kids at once.

When my college friends were talking about having kids, all the thoughts, literally all of them, swirled in my brain, jumping between my subconscious and conscious mind. They did all the talking, and I did all the listening. I don't recall ever saying anything or anyone asking me directly. One day, I was in the shower singing along to whatever was on the radio, and it hit me — I knew I didn't want to have any children. Being as direct as I am, I immediately shared this with my parents, who seemed more stunned than anything. With blank stares, they both managed to say, "Okay."

My parents have usually been supportive of what I do, even if they don't entirely agree with it. I was a little surprised that they were okay with my decision. They literally just looked at me and said, "Okay," and life went on. When I was dating in my late 20s and 30s, my mom did express that it would be more challenging for me to date since I didn't want to have children. So what? I didn't smoke, rarely drank, and it was what it was.

Here's where I need to pause and explain what I see as the difference between *childless* and *child-free*. Being child-free is an accepted choice, as in my case, where I obviously don't want to have kids.

Being childless is not a choice. To me, this is when you want to have children but you literally and/or medically are unable to have kids for whatever reason.

I once made the mistake of assuming someone who didn't have children was child-free and was quickly advised they were childless, and that one conversation was a pivotal one. I now no longer presume those without children are child-free as they may be childless. I do hope they are happy even though they could not have the family they had envisioned

Once I made this life-altering decision, I pretty much stepped into adulthood. I knew I needed to find my own circles of friends and colleagues, since I would not be part of the world that allows for "automatic access" to other adults. I wouldn't be taking a child to school, or scouts, or athletic practices and games.

Despite having that feeling that I was destined to become an office administrator or executive assistant, I knew I wanted a career compiled of more than one income source. Someone I knew through a college friend told me about the entrepreneurship program they were in and that the school had stopped offering it the year before I started attending. However, it piqued my interest, and I started to pursue entrepreneurship after graduation.

I also knew that being an entrepreneur, working more than one job, and following career goals didn't leave much time for raising children.

In 2006, I created my first social community via Meetup.com. That summer I started two South Shore groups. I then went on to create and build two more Meetup groups. The South Shore Dining Out Meetup group is the only one that is still active. As I type this in the Summer of 2023, I realize that I started three groups 17 years ago in 2006-2008 and that we nearly lost the South Shore Dining Out Meetup group a couple of times. I had stepped away for a few years, and a friend kept it going for me. Someone literally asked me right as I was in the midst of typing this if I meet a lot of single people through the group. While I do, it's not my main reason for running the group. My main reason is the reason I started it — to dine out with and meet other adults at various restaurants on the South Shore of Massachusetts.

In my early to mid-20s, I worked both a full-time job as well as a part-time job. Then I lost my full-time job, and that's how my entrepreneurial journey began. Fast forward to my late 20s when I fell into a career in Property & Casualty Insurance. In less than three years, I had both a designation and my insurance license. Less than a decade after that, in 2018, I made my best decision ever — I got my Real Estate Salesperson's License and began working more with my dad. Despite a couple of stumbling blocks, I went full time in January 2019 and haven't looked back. In the fall of 2023, barely over four years later, I earned my Real Estate Broker's License — which is as high as you can go. I am now licensed in both P&C Insurance and Real Estate in the state of MA.

Both of these careers are 100% relationship-based.

Communities are extremely important in both my personal and professional life.

And I wanted to build more new communities to build personal and professional relationships.

In February 2016 I joined Toastmasters, and a few months later dove head-first and went all-in. I have met hundreds of Toastmasters not just in Massachusetts and Rhode Island, but worldwide, as I attended the International Convention in 2018. Toastmasters is one of my favorite organizations. I enjoy both personal and professional growth and development. I enjoy helping others. I enjoy learning. I enjoy getting to know my fellow Club members as well as other Toastmasters locally and around the world. My club was there for me during a challenging time, and my leadership in the club and (even more so) in the district has been a great experience and enabled me to make and maintain many friendships. I can remember when I was an Area Director in 2018-2019, and three of the four clubs in my area always made me feel welcome every time I visited, constantly thanking and inviting me to keep coming back. I still keep in touch with several members of those clubs to this day. While Toastmasters does accomplish its mission with me, it does so much more as it is a friend circle for me as well.

In April 2018, I officially joined Rotary, a month shy of my dad's 40th Anniversary as a Rotarian. Two months later, the incoming club President appointed me as the Youth Services Committee Chair. This made sense, since I was the student founder of my high school Interact Club, which falls under Youth Services. Dad joined the Braintree Rotary Club about a month before I was born. I grew up going to many Rotary events and taking part in service projects with my Dad. Braintree Rotary has always been family to me. As I got older I sometimes went to things without dad. Sometimes when he would introduce me as his guest, he would say, "My daughter Angela brought me as her guest," which always elicited laughter in the air at the meetings and still brings a smile to my face to this day. Now, five plus years into my lifelong Rotary membership, as I learn more, do more, and meet more members both in the club, locally, and worldwide, I know Rotary is always going to welcome me, regardless of whether or not I bring my dad to a meeting.

Summer 2019 was pivotal in my Commercial Real Estate community building. We were invited by a Referral Partner of my dad's to do work in a specific town. One of my friends had been inviting me to a networking group in that town for a few years. I connected with her, and less than a month later, there we were — my dad, one of our associates, and me — at a Networking Group USA (aka NGU) meeting. This chapter had 25+ members, and three to four guests were always at their meetings. Dad turned to me that fall after we joined and basically said, "You know what's next, right?" to which I blindly replied, "What?" His answer was, "We need to start a chapter more local to our hometown and geographical niche area." While we did so as a team, we also did this with the focus of building my business network.

NGU was the catalyst for several reasons, one in particular. First, they met twice a month for one hour and encouraged 1:1 meetings beyond that. Second, the requirements were simple enough, in my opinion — attend four to six meetings per quarter, and you can send a sub. Third, the cost was super reasonable — $75 per calendar year. Fourth, I met a business coach with whom I have been working since Spring 2021 and without whom I wouldn't have been able to dive headfirst into this book project. In one of our coaching sessions, I mentioned some ideas to him, and he loved the child-free angle and then put it together with community, and that's how this story came to be.

My business coach is Don Wilson of Prospecting Intelligence. He took Dad's referral partner strategy and ran with it with me. He gave me easy-to-follow steps, and being the rule-follower teacher's pet that I am, I ran with it, too. Within six months, I had 20 Referral Partners in 15 businesses. They are a solid mix of golden referral partner sources, silver referral partner sources, and neither of those, although most are in the golden and silver categories comprising the overwhelming majority.

My community building continues now, albeit at a slightly slower pace. Other communities I have joined and been part of for three or more years effectively as of Summer 2023 include:

- Polka Dot Powerhouse, a sisterhood of uplifting positive abundant women in the US, Canada, and the UK (with hopefully more countries to follow in the next few years)

- SheBreathes Collaborative, with whom I am collaborating on writing this story for their anthology and which I joined in the Fall of 2020, during the pandemic. I love being able to meet women who are not traditional, or who are traditional but have some non-traditional businesses, values, or ways of doing business. Some have become good friends, while others are acquaintances and business associates. I have utilized some of their services and am building community and connections with others via one-to-one meetings and attending Collaborative meetings and other events at the WeBreathe Wellness space. It's a place I can go and be me without judgment which is always a welcome feeling.

- Boston Business Women, a Facebook community of 40K+ in New England primarily focused on business building and lifting each other up. This group originally was a Boston-area-based group, and not long after I became involved, in mid-2021 it expanded to include all of New England. There are several sub-groups representing non-MA states as well as different regions/areas of MA. I am a BBW Inner Circle Member, an Affiliate, and a Co-Moderator of the BBW South Shore Facebook Group. Several of my Referral Partners I met through the BBW.

- Chambers of Commerce — Dad has been part of the South Shore Chamber of Commerce since I was a kid. I visited a few times in the past and became active in 2019. We also joined several other Chambers and Business Associations in which I became active. The Cranberry Country Chamber of Commerce was a pivotal one for me in 2020 and 2021. I feel like I'm "home" there and get to see people who know me and my business as well as meet new people. During COVID, those who attended the 3rd Friday virtual networking lunches really got to know each other, both personally and professionally. We were all in the same boat — "stuck" at home, shifting to working and meeting virtually 95-100% of the time as opposed to 33% of the time. We were able to go into parts of each other's homes and lives that we otherwise would not have been able to do so pre-Covid. It changed part of the way I do business and part of how I interact with others, both personally and professionally.

My life is full, rich, and rewarding.

While I get to do many things with ease, it does have its challenges.

I don't choose friends based on whether or not they have kids. Although, those who do not have kids have more flexibility and time freedom than those who do not. They may have other interests like mine. However, they know who to call to talk to, as I love to talk and am a great listener as well (which I have been told by several people so don't take my word for it!).

I'm also a podcast host. I started my podcast, Talking Toastmasters, in the fall of 2020 and launched it on January 5th, 2021. I get to do this with my cousin/godson, William Tarashuk, who is both a podcast host a couple of times over as well as my mentor and producer. Each episode, on average, takes about two and a half to three hours between recording, editing playback, a few other behind-the-scenes items, and promoting it. I then spend another hour or two or several weeks on other aspects of the podcast. It's both a labor of love and a love of learning about and meeting new people, hearing about their Toastmasters experiences, and sharing them with the world. District 31 Toastmasters has been extremely supportive of my podcast as well. Shoutout to District 31 for being my first and loyal sponsor.

As you can see, communities and finding my "tribe" and/or "people" who accept us are really important to me both personally and professionally.

There are many titles in my life that I enjoy. Daughter. Bestie. Friend. Cousin. Rotarian. Toastmaster. Distinguished Toastmaster. Founder. Mentor. Real Estate Broker. Sister. While the only "mother" title I will have in my lifetime is that of godmother, I am more than okay with that.

Angela Nuss is an outgoing extrovert, happily single, and child-, pet-, and consumer debt-free condo owner. She loves Disney, dining out, traveling, cultivating friendships, tennis, walking, and investing several hours per week in health and wellness programs.

In 2018, Angela joined Rotary International after being an "honorary" member since birth. She is also a Distinguished Toastmaster who has been a member of Toastmasters International since 2016.

As a licensed real estate broker with Jay Nuss Realty Group, LLC, Angela works with property owners, business owners, and investors in Eastern MA.

As an independent property and casualty insurance agent, she works in her client's best interests by partnering with agencies both within MA and nationwide. She is also a notary in Massachusetts.

Angela's vision statement is "to leave the world a better place. I believe that women should be able to achieve happiness, health, wealth, love, and acceptance by leading an authentic life."

BETH KNAUS

THE WEIGHT OF CHOICE

It was Thanksgiving, 1994. My ex-husband and I were heading to New York to see our families, anxious to announce that I was pregnant. I asked my mother-in-law to invite my mother for dinner, because I knew she didn't have anywhere to go. When my mother arrived, my ex and I pulled her aside to tell her privately that I was pregnant. With a blank stare, she said, "Congratulations," then turned and walked away.

For the rest of the night, everyone else fawned over us, asking all the typical questions — due date, name choices, boy or girl, how I was feeling, etc. My own mother said nothing. I could see the other guests stealing glances at each other and at my mother. She contributed nothing but awkward silence. It was embarrassing, infuriating, baffling, and mostly, disappointing.

We went home to Boston. Six weeks passed, and my mother did not call me one time. Her only child, pregnant with her first grandchild. I wrote a letter telling her how upset I was, that I would not have my kids grow up with this type of toxic abuse, that she would not hurt them the way she had hurt me, that she had abused me, my dad, and other people around her emotionally and physically because of her alcoholism. I told her if she got sober, I'd be willing to work on our relationship and have her be a part of our family. I was 28. We never spoke again.

I know some readers will see me as heartless for cutting off my own mother. It's rare, I know. Most people would rather suffer the consequences of abuse than to take that step. And I do not judge them. This is a "do not try this at home" scenario.

If I had cut off my father, people might say, "Men! Good for you. That no-good bastard doesn't deserve to be in your life."

Okay, maybe that's a little dramatic. But it's a much more common attitude. When I look back at my life, I'm stunned by the relatives and friends my parents had who knew what was happening and chose to defend, protect, and feel bad for her. "She's your mother," they would say. No one spoke up and said, "What's going on isn't right." I was a kid living in a chronically dysfunctional alcoholic home for years, and my "family" chose to look the other way.

Here's how I got to this point.

As a child, both of my parents were alcoholics – functional in that our house was clean and we ate well, thanks to my mother. And we had a roof over our heads thanks to my dad, and summer vacations and presents under the tree.

Weekends were party time for my parents. Cocktails with

neighbors, Saturday nights out dancing and drinking with friends. I was an only child and spent lots of time entertaining myself. I loved nothing more than a Saturday night with my two enchanting babysitting sisters from next door. They were blonde, blue-eyed, and beautiful, so caring and kind, and it made me feel cool and special like I belonged.

I learned at a young age, that after drink number two, my mother was delightful, witty, and pseudo-charming. For instance, she might ask me to sit nice and close to her on the neighbor's patio so she could put her arm around me and call me "Hun." But that third drink pushed her into the angry zone.

The insults would start flying, aimed at anyone in the room. Like when I was fourteen and holding my boyfriend's hand on the living room couch and she called me a slut. Or telling me my father was gay and having an affair with his best friend, which was not true. And letting my aunt know that if she would stick to the latest diet, she wouldn't be so fat. My mother was a stealthy instigator, picking fights out of thin air, sometimes between two other people. Hearing ice cubes in a cocktail glass can still take me back there.

My dad stopped drinking when I was seven. I was too young to understand, so I had no idea what had changed, and why my parents weren't going out on weekends anymore, why a chasm grew between them, and why my mother's unhappiness intensified.

She became jealous of how close my father and I were. When he wasn't around, I got scolded and punished for no reason, just something she fabricated. I learned how to move quietly and stay out of her sight. But she would find me in our small ranch, bait me into arguments, and then punish me.

When my dad got home, she would tell him why I was punished. I would plead with him to remove the punishment, but he told me he had to honor what she said because he wasn't here to see for himself. One time when my dad came home, she told him what I had done, and she demanded that he be the one to spank me. She knew how painful it would be for both him and me to have to go through that. I remember him apologizing afterward with tears in his eyes.

Her bitterness grew into physical and emotional abuse towards both of us. She was a public face smacker — at family events, or if I had friends over, or if we had company at the house or if I said something she thought would make people think badly of her as a parent. I had developed some stealthy Keanu Reeves *Matrix* skills, but she would get me on the second or third attempt. She was determined to make contact.

My father handled her so calmly, with patience and compassion, which was confusing and frustrating for me. Why was he so kind when she was so mean? Her behavior became increasingly volatile and unpredictable.

When I was around 11 years old, my father told me that he was a recovering alcoholic and that the nights he said he was at his second job, he was actually at Alcoholics Anonymous meetings. He explained that he was trying to get my mother to go too, that her behaviors were due to the disease of alcoholism, that she was sick and it wasn't who she really was. So he started to bring me with him to meetings.

She would do things like take a knife to bed with her and tell me I had better stay awake or she would kill my father when he got home. I fell asleep on the rug by the front door, waiting for him. He made plans once to go on a weekend retreat with some friends from A.A. My mother didn't leave "the compound" often, and she didn't want him to leave, either. So she cut up his clothes so he wouldn't have any to pack for the trip.

I saw her hit my father many times, once repeatedly with the handle of the corded phone in our kitchen. She threw a boiling hot pot of soup over the brand-new dining room table when my dad told her he was taking me out to eat. She was full of rage and wanted us to know.

But the thing that hurt me the most was losing my best friend when I was around 10 years old. My mother drunk-dialed my friend's mom to brag about my report card, say how much smarter I was, and that her daughter was lucky that I was friends with her. They exchanged words, my mother said something racist and horrible, and my friend was forbidden to spend any time with me after that. My mother told me it happened because of something I did to upset my friend's mother. I lived with that for over 40 years, until I reconnected with my friend a few years ago and she told me the truth.

When I was 15, my parents got divorced. I want you to think about the time frame. It's 1981. I'm 15 years old. My parents were divorced. My father told my mother to leave. And I as a young teenage girl was living with my dad. None of these things were common at the time. But I was so relieved she was gone.

My dad encouraged me to have a relationship with my mother. I know he felt horrible that I did not have an attentive, loving, and kind role model. He wanted me to visit with her and buy her nice cards on her birthday and Mother's Day. I know he also wanted her to mother me.

The truth is, my mother was dutiful. I was well dressed, well fed, and well mannered. But I did not know her. I don't know what her childhood was like or what her dreams were. I do not know how she and my father met. We did not go out to lunch or do special mother-and-daughter things. She did not paint my nails for me or show me how to put lipstick on. We did not play Barbies together or go to the playground. And she certainly did not teach me anything about my body and becoming a woman. It was my father who took me for my first bra fitting while the women there looked at him suspiciously. He went to buy my "lady supplies," and later would pick up my birth control prescription. My mother addressed her responsibilities as a mother and nothing more — without an ounce of warmth, connection, or nurturing.

I remember sitting on her lap and her pushing me off, saying, "Get off of me, it's too hot." Or, "You'll wrinkle my dress." As I got older, if I went to hug and kiss her, she would put her hands up on my biceps or shoulders to avoid the closeness, then offer me her cheek.

After the divorce, her family turned their backs on us, initially defending her. My dad and I had Thanksgiving alone that first year. Even though I was with my favorite person at my favorite restaurant, I was so sad. Every year, I hunt for someone, a "stray" we affectionately call them, to sit at our holiday table who has nowhere else to go or can't be with their family. No one will feel like we felt at that dinner if I can help it.

After that, people from my dad's AA family became our family. He would drop me off with his close friend Gerry so she could talk about all the girl things with me. I met one of my closest friends in AA. I could talk to anyone there about anything and know that they would keep my secrets, even from my dad. It's probably the place I have felt the safest in my life, along with the home I live in now.

When I graduated college with a degree in small business management, of which she did not contribute a dime, my mother went to Florida instead. I was the first generation to actually go to college, and she chose not to be there. When I got engaged, she said, "I don't know why you're getting married. You'll only get divorced." I stayed in a marriage, which, in my opinion, was an abusive and taxing relationship, way too long because I did not want her to be right.

She was embarrassed to tell her friends that I was a hairdresser, even though I worked hard and made more money than she did. So she kept offering me a job at her bank so that she could brag about my having a "respectable" job. I owned a hair salon in Boston by the time I was 23. That wasn't good enough, either.

I rarely shared my situation with other people, especially other women. I can certainly understand how women treasure their relationships with their mothers. But they usually can't understand that not everyone's mother is wonderful and how having no relationship with my mother was a better choice for me. I have had to defend my choice many times, because others just can't fathom not being involved with their mothers. But my mother was not their mother.

When my mother died in 2009, she still had the letter I sent, and alcohol in her refrigerator. I was surprised by my disappointment, and I realized somewhere in my protective walls, I had always carried that little hope that she would change. But her choice was not mine to make. Not going to lie: I was relieved that it was over. Every day from the time I sent that letter, I had checked in with myself to see if I still felt right in my choice. Every day, that answer was yes.

Distance has allowed me to have some empathy and understanding. My mother was bright and worked in the city when my parents met. I think she wanted a career instead of kids, something women still struggle with. When I say this, people will say, "Oh, of course she wanted you. Of course, she loved you." But it was the early 1960s, and she did what was expected of women at that time — she met a man who could provide for her, put a roof over her head, and work hard so she could stay at home to raise children.

My children never met her. My oldest daughter just turned 28, and it really hit me that she is now the age I was when I made that difficult choice.

When I got pregnant with my first, my in-laws had five grandsons, and I wanted a girl so badly. My wish came true. Then I had a second beautiful daughter and a beautiful son. Motherhood has been an incredibly healing journey for me. I'd like to think I've been a more loving, encouraging, and positive mother than my mother was.

Despite not having a maternal connection, I feel fortunate in a number of ways.

My dad's choice to get sober was the best choice he ever made for himself and for me. For 42 years, he was my solid — the one adult I could trust and rely on. He taught me things that you normally wouldn't learn from your mother, like advocating for yourself, speaking directly about uncomfortable subjects, being real and truthful, and accepting yourself and your flaws. Being raised by him gave me a different perspective, and that has helped me to get where I am today.

AA taught me the real definition of "family" — the people you can rely on, those who show up for you when no one else will. It has nothing to do with blood or water.

I had close relationships with the moms of two good friends of mine who generously shared their mothers with me. Houses I could show up at and get fed and feel safe, even today. I have passed this on, not only through having seats at my table for anyone who needs one but by welcoming my kids' friends into our home and our life when they needed it.

Here's my message to you. If you're being hurt, disrespected, or abused by someone in your life, you have the choice to live with it or not. But you have to be clear on both that choice and its consequences. Build yourself a community of friends and family who love and support you. Then trust that you are the only one who can make the best choice for you. You don't need anyone's approval to love and care for yourself.

Beth Knaus is a copywriter, brand messaging consultant, and owner of That's A Spade Copywriting Services. She loves writing and the challenge of crafting bold and clear messaging for clients ready to tell a deeper story to reach the right audience.

Beth has been writing since she was young — journaling, poetry, essays, and short stories, some which have been published in group anthologies. She is currently working on a memoir. To read more of her personal work, you can find her on Medium, a platform for writers.

You can learn more about Beth at: www.thatsaspade.com

Becky

BECKY BAST

A JUMBLED ADHD PATH
TO BECOMING A DECLUTTERER

AROUND 2016

I was a mom on the go, living the minivan mom-bomb life. Iced coffee at the ready, ideally the perfect '90s hip hop song on the radio, the kids happily chatting in the backseat. Maya four, Jojo two. What could be better? The whole day ahead of us to go to the park, go to some random play area. Hopefully, I'd get to talk to other parents who are socially needy. Who can actually stay in the house all day? Sure it's easier in some ways — easier to keep track of two little ones and a dog, and nap schedules to maintain. But I might lose my mind.

Hold up! Cruising down the road, I did a double take, rubbernecking, frothing at the mouth at the sight of that hideous Little Tikes play structure on the side of the road. That must be hundreds of dollars, and it's free! I can entertain my kids and save my family money! I'm a rockstar! I was kinda self-conscious that it was on the street where I grew up. My family might be horrified to see me stuffing this beast into my amazing yet crumb-ridden, hearty minivan. Man, what a rush.

As a married, stay-at-home mom living on one income in a wealthy suburb, I had pride and enjoyment in saving my family money. Hand me down clothes, toys, you name it. Savers on 50-percent off days was like Christmickah. A whole new wardrobe for $100!

Here's how I went from a mom pulling a u-ey to grab free items off the side of the road, to the Declutterista, diagnosed with ADHD at 41, and helping myself and others get their life decluttered.

Somehow *The Art of Tidying Up* landed in my house. I remember leaning over my kitchen counter and reading a few pages. I got the gist that the best way to tidy up was to create categories of items. Take out all of the clothes at once and go through them to see what items brought joy to you and then thank them for serving you. I rushed through my house like a tornado, saying heck no to categories, but quickly asking myself, does it bring me joy? Quick decisions were made. Bags of clothes, toys, and housewares were clustered. There was a rush of collecting these items, then I loaded up that pile of donations and dumped the items off at Savers. I was diagnosed with anxiety and depression in my 20s. However, during this decluttering process, my anxiety dissipated, and I felt lighter and free, with valuable brain space cleared in my head.

I was hooked and wanted more productive and satisfying fun like this. I asked friends if I could help them declutter. I remember having a blast going through my friend's kitchen cabinets. We joked with her teenage son that this was how adults had fun. Pretty sad, huh? She was very supportive and said, "You have something here, Becky."

I remember getting together with a couple of childhood friends. The host was all about me decluttering her mudroom. I felt pressured and agreed. But my best friend assured me that I could choose to be "Becky the friend" when I wanted, and not always the declutterer. This made me realize my hyperfocus and my low-key obsession, and it also deflated me. Didn't she understand that I had found my thing?

Before discovering this passion for going through people's stuff to make their lives easier and better, and figuring out what they need and what they love, I knew I wanted the flexibility to be there for my children, satisfy my social needs, and help out our family financially.

I don't remember knowing what I wanted to do when I grew up. Being social, likable, having fun, and making others laugh came naturally to me. My academic family gave me the push, focus, and confidence to see what my talents were and which ones made sense for college and my future career. Since I had no chosen path, I shrugged and thought, "OK, sure that makes sense," trusting their suggestions.

1998

I applied for early decision and got into Mount Holyoke, a beautiful and apparently prestigious school. Phew, that was easy. I couldn't really figure out which major fulfilled the need to get a job, excel at it, and enjoy it. I played on the college tennis team for a few years which was thrilling to both me and my dad, who worked so hard to encourage me since age eight to keep playing tennis. Although he passed away five years ago, I know he would be excited that my kids were taking lessons on the very same cracked court where I used to practice with him. He told me it was a lifelong sport, and although I probably rolled my eyes, I am actually on a tennis team and play competitively now in my 40s.

2003

After college, I lived with five other roommates. I was lost and baffled by how people got up every morning and do the same thing. My mom thought that since we have some of the best hospitals in the country right here in the Boston area, she encouraged me to look at health care. As an overweight but healthy lifestyle person, I was interested in how to overcome obesity and embrace healthy living in general. I got an entry-level job at Children's Hospital and slowly moved up administratively. My parents had also called Emerson College to discover there was a perfect new program for me. Health Communications.

"You have an interest in health, and you are good at communications," they said. I was told I was very creative and a great writer with a lot of potential if I only reworked my writing and edited it. The classic story about me is that when my first-grade teacher asked me to redo an assignment, I told her I only do things once. That doesn't really seem like me because I am a people pleaser, but the story was told multiple times, so it must be true. I shrugged again and decided to apply for the health communications degree while being an administrative assistant for neurologists at Children's Hospital.

It was my first time balancing work and school. When I look

back now, I don't think I gave it 110 percent. My mom suggested I try development at the hospital. I didn't know what development or fundraising entailed, but it was quite a large operation at Children's, with over a hundred people doing more than simply calling people on the phone and asking for money. I thought the field was interesting, was happy about the mission, and my colleagues were fun and bright. My boss assumed I would pick up on this new job quickly because she was impressed by the college I attended. Although she was known to be Devil Wears Prada-ish, she told me I had a great attitude.

That was similar to the feedback my tennis coach, who also cut me from the team after two years, gave me. "You're not really improving, but we really liked your personality,." they said. I eventually moved up a bit in fundraising with a supportive, laid-back team. I never felt like I excelled at the administrative jobs, but I liked leaving at 5 p.m.

2012

When I got pregnant, I was told that I would need to be a working mom because I had a lot of social needs. At 2 a.m. one morning, while I was on maternity leave, I woke up my husband and told him I wanted to be a stay-at-home mom. My 90-minute commute from Franklin to Boston did not bring him joy, and my salary barely covered more than the cost of daycare. Since he worked closer to home, he knew he was going to be stuck doing more of the errands and pick-ups. I remember being nervous to tell my parents about my new SAHM status. They worked so hard to put me through a private prestigious school, and they were still paying it off years later. My mom was very chill and told me she just wanted me to have choices in life. I breathed a quick sigh of relief. Now to break the news to work.

I knew I had a purpose to help others and lead my best life. I dabbled in various network marketing companies, including Beachbody, one for frozen food prep, and Touchstone Jewelry. I never wore jewelry, but now I was selling it. Yes, because I wanted community, connection, flexible hours, and money. I could be successful if I worked hard. I didn't mind putting myself out there and talking to people about products and services, but I didn't like the admin piece. Learning their systems was tedious and a bit overwhelming.

MAYBE 2015

At a playdate, one of my mom friends mentioned she had a big job before kids and said she was really into podcasts. I didn't know what that was, but I quickly downloaded various podcasts on entrepreneur topics and self-help. These were a game changer. With two little kids and a puppy, I didn't have the time or mental capacity to read actual books.

I think around this time I also thought, aha! I could be a life coach. I liked to work on people's mental health, I liked to give people ideas on how to live their best life. I felt like my life had a lot of possibilities and I was meant to be an entrepreneur. Someone actually said to me, "What do you know about life? You're overweight." Although I haven't pursued a program in coaching yet, I have never dropped the idea and still consider it.

I believe podcasts inspired me to become a morning person. I loved going to the gym with my mom and sister and having Starbucks while my family was still asleep. I had time to gather myself before the cute but crazy storm of kid, puppy, and husband needs. I thought I maybe could have my own podcast someday.

2017

For some reason, I jump in and don't overthink certain things. Decluttering seemed to check all the boxes. I thought it was fun, I was good at it, I had no problem putting myself out there, and people's eyes lit up when I told them what I did.

I thought the best way to get myself out there fast would be to create a Facebook business page. It took minutes and I had a cool name, The Declutterista. While I was creating this business, I learned about a company in beta testing called Pepperlane. It was mostly for moms to create their own businesses on their terms. I went there to support my sister's new business but walked away excited to create an easy website through Pepperlane for my own decluttering business. My talented photographer friend took some lovely shots for me, and there it was. My best friend's girlfriend created a sparkly teal logo that really spoke to me.

PROBABLY 2018

I became a Pepperlane networking leader and enjoyed supporting and promoting other female entrepreneurs. I got my name out there with decluttering lectures, donating my services to auctions, having booths at events, finding networking opportunities like at SheBreathes, posting photos and videos related to mental health, and decluttering. I hired a few business coaches who helped me stay focused and learn to charge my worth. The actual decluttering was and still is a blast. I felt comfortable going into people's homes. They felt at ease with me, and I loved to be useful by showing them a powerful and lighter end result.

My superpower is making people comfortable, meeting them where they are, and matching their energy. I don't have a set way to do things, because everyone is different and I try to customize my services. I was often just the right amount of busy to enjoy my children and fulfill my entrepreneurial dreams.

2019

The opportunity to start a podcast fell in my lap when I met a woman who owned a podcast studio. Sure, I could figure out how to technologically do my own, but here you showed up, recorded, and they did the editing. I decided to call my podcast "Lighten Up With the Declutterista". It was a mix of random *Curb Your Enthusiasm*-type moments from my random and awkward life, an interview with another entrepreneur, and some decluttering tips.

This format required minimal preparation. I could jot down a few things before the show and go with it. Planning and following a set script made me more nervous. I met so many great people from networking, so I had plenty of guests for my show. I even had a new logo and an original song created for the podcast. It was fun, easy, high-level, and only $200 a month. I helped others promote their businesses, and they had fun being my podcast guests. I think if I showcased my decluttering more, perhaps I would have gotten clients because of the podcast, but I didn't want it to feel like work. I started to think of ways to make money from the podcast but decided to transition to community TV. It was free, they did all the work, and I could have a similar format with a time restriction.

I was all set to have my first show, but there was a virus going around called Covid so I got nervous. Then the world shut down. I focused on whatever we all did with our little kids, — adjusting and trying to do the best we could with the new restrictions on life. My family looks back with fond memories of this time — watching a new movie every day, me educating them on '80s and '90s pop culture, daily McFlurries, hiking, going to the beach, and garage holidays with the family. I tried some virtual decluttering sessions, but it didn't stick. I lost my decluttering mojo and that was OK at the time. I focused on getting through the day as best as possible. It's a blur in time for many of us, and although someone close to us was in the ICU with Covid, we came out unscathed.

ADHD DIAGNOSIS

I think after college I was wandering like a dandelion in the wind. Trying hard to enjoy my life. My older sister said, "You work so hard to be happy, but you're not. I think you should look into medication." I'm pretty sure I was in therapy at this point. I got diagnosed with anxiety and depression and went on Celexa.

2022

Fast forward 20 years, when I read an article that many women were misdiagnosed with depression and anxiety but actually had ADHD. After balking at the idea of getting tested due to my "what's the point" attitude and financial concern, I found a realistic option. I took the TOVA test, also known as the most boring computer game ever, and I definitely scored high with ADHD.

When I asked about the ADHD testing, I told the psychologist you wouldn't believe what I do for work — declutter and organize. She thought it made perfect sense, because people with ADHD can hyper-focus. The ADHD diagnosis helped explain my habits in school — I was a pretty good student but goofed off in class. I always had to ask friends on the phone what the homework was. I didn't really know how to study efficiently. I'm always going for that dopamine hit, whether it's food, coffee, a new idea, a new interest, or a new friend. I'm very restless and moody. I realized that I can get overstimulated. It's very hard for me to sit still and be present. I've always binged periodically, definitely overate, and struggled to keep up with systems. I hate the words consistency and routine, because they are just things I won't be able to keep up with. I do think ADHD has given me the courage to jump into many things, have an interesting life, be open to possibilities, and have an understanding of myself and others due to empathy and sensitivity.

The downside for me is that I'm easily addicted to things and can be moody. It's a real challenge for me to stick to new things, and I find it hard to be present especially at home, because home feels like a to-do list. I'm a morning person, but my mental energy is often fried in the afternoon when I'm with my kids, so I constantly feel like I'm not enough, whether it's as a cook or listener, having the energy to play with kids, and getting overstimulated easily.

I think I was happy and kind of obsessed with this diagnosis. It seemed more desirable than depression and anxiety. I think I went off Celexa and Wellbutrin and went on Adderall. I thought it was a game changer at first, but I got headaches and experienced huge energy crashes and intense moods.

I always thought it would be fun to work at my fave daily spot, Starbucks, but I always thought that it looked too hard. The perfect combination of it never being open and my Adderall courage motivated me to apply, and I worked there for four months. It was enjoyable and I'm glad I tried it. But I wasn't catching on, and it didn't work for my family's lifestyle.

2023

I got my decluttering spark back and I'm busier than ever. My TV show is on the air, I play on a tennis team, and I'm still able to prioritize my family. My life is messy. My house can be messy, but it's pretty decluttered, so it's easier to clean up.

I'm a declutterer or organizer with an ADHD diagnosis. Many of my clients struggled with it and I could relate, but my executive functioning didn't hold me back totally from household tasks and adulting. However, I would declutter and clean, but it seemed pretty much impossible for me to keep systems in my house and car. First, I have a family that is generally not tidy. Second, when my brain is toast, I don't have it in me.

In my early decluttering days, I was not a fan of containers. They had so much promise and appeal, but you need to declutter first. I realized I really need containers to maintain my systems. Looking back at my life, I think that the not always appreciated guidance of loved ones and my willingness to say OK to please them led me to a solid foundation or container, if you will. I'm decluttering parts of my life that don't work but creating my own type of container.

STRENGTHS OF BEING A MOM WITH ADHD

I'm not afraid to ask for help when I need it, I am real and honest with my kids, and I speak my thoughts because it's hard not to. I love doing fun and interesting things, I support my kids' interests, and I'm good at many things. I'm also an excellent problem solver.

THINGS I'VE LEARNED ALONG THE WAY THAT WORK FOR ME AS A MOM AND ENTREPRENEUR WITH ADHD:

- Ask for help. Even if you do not have the financial means to hire people, figure out a way.

- Flow is what comes naturally when doing what you enjoy and get paid for it.

- People are rarely thinking about you. Try not to care about what others think. No one thinks you look fat, etc., and if they do, they will go right back to thinking about themselves and their own issues.

- Make yourself proud. External gratification and always seeking approval are exhausting.

- Give yourself and others a break — they are doing the best they can (I'm working on this myself).

- Figure out how to make life fun. I am probably having more fun than ever.

- If you have an idea, don't wait until all your ducks are in a row. Test it out and put yourself out there.

- Do something you enjoy every day.

- Learn how to say YES and no. Establish healthy boundaries.

- Be vulnerable, but with the right people.

- Be comfortable in your own skin no matter which side of you shows up. Don't get pressured into being who you are not.

- Trust yourself.

- Spend time in nature.

- Hide your phone! Always having mine increased my anxiety, ADHD, mom guilt, eye-sight, and irritability.

- Stop the dieting hamster wheel. I've tried them all and gained the weight back. Now I am trying to eat certain foods to help my ADHD and moods and to break my addiction to sugary coffee drinks.

- Try to give yourself a break, even if it means hiding in the bathroom, before you lose it.

Becky Bast is the one and only Declutterista! She's also a wife and a mom, and lives with her hubby, her two kids, and the family's golden puppy, Bob, in Sharon, MA. She enjoys sitting at Starbucks, playing tennis, karaoke, concerts, and of course, decluttering.

She has tried everything from skydiving to stand-up comedy, but also loves driving and listening to Taylor Swift or '90s hip hop.

You can learn more about Becky at: www.declutterista.com

Cathy

CATHY RIPLEY GREENE

THE DAY I COULD HAVE DIED BUT I DIDN'T

The last thing I remember seeing is the rear wheel of a really big truck as it got closer and closer.

I don't remember much after that until I heard the screaming. It was loud and shrill and I wanted it to stop. Then I realized I was the one screaming.

It was Sunday, October 22nd, 2017, the day I could have died, but I didn't.

I was lying on my back in the emergency room at the Rhode Island Hospital in Providence with no awareness of what had happened, how I ended up in the ER, or why I was screaming. My husband Craig was by my side and he explained that I had been in a serious motorcycle accident. I was attended to by multiple doctors and nursing staff. As it turns out, I needed to have a chest tube placed to help inflate a portion of my lung that had collapsed, thus, the screaming. If you haven't had an emergency chest tube procedure while wide awake, I promise it's not something you want to experience.

We had been enjoying a beautiful afternoon motorcycle ride and were returning to the bike shop to buy the bike I was test riding. I was happy, excited, and feeling good. We were at a red light in the far left lane. A semi tractor-trailer pulled up next to me, also turning left. Craig was riding in front of me and we were communicating through our com system. I remember telling him that a "big truck just pulled up next to me."

"Just look up the road where you are headed," he reminded me. As an experienced rider, he was supporting the development of good riding habits in me, a newer motorcyclist.

The light turned green, I pulled in the clutch, first gear, feet off the ground, let off the brakes, gave it some throttle, and onward I went. What I failed to do was turn my head and look where I was going. Instead, I fixated on the truck and drove the bike straight into the rear wheels and the side of the semi. At the time I had no awareness of what was happening. My husband told me later that he realized I was not negotiating the turn and he began screaming my name, "CATHY! CATHY! CATHY!" to get my attention, but I did not hear a thing. It was as if I was not in my body, like I was somewhere else, and my mind had disconnected from all things physical and mental until right before I hit.

That's when I saw the wheel in front of me, and said out loud, calmly and peacefully, "Oh God."

Just then, there was a beautiful, soft light. I felt peaceful, "suspended." Then I felt nothing. Craig saw the accident in its entirety. I imagine, in a way, that his psychological injury is greater than the totality of my physical injuries. Speaking of those, here's my list:

Twenty-six fractures that included fourteen ribs fractured in multiple places, six transverse processes of the spine fractured, one clavicle, the right shoulder in two spots, one finger, and two bones in the foot. A punctured right lung, multiple tendon tears, a concussion, skin abrasions, muscle strains, and one complete and total mind blown.

Craig told me he did not know how anyone could survive what he watched me go through. He saw me hitting the wheels and the side of the truck, getting tangled with the bike, sliding and rolling under the truck, hitting the stabilizer bar at the front of the truck, and then coming to a stop face down in the street, under the truck. He thought I was dead.

Thankfully, the driver of the truck realized something had happened and stopped mid-turn. Had he not, well, it's pretty clear I would not be here.

How am I still alive? I wonder about that, I mean, after all, I rode a motorcycle into the rear wheels of a semi-tractor trailer.

Five days in the intensive care unit (ICU) was followed by five days in the step-down unit and then one week in a rehabilitation center, where I gained a bit of mobility and strength so I could return home to recover.

We welcomed into our home the visiting nurse association, an occupational therapist, a physical therapist, a case worker, supportive equipment, and a gathering of family and friends all offering their help and support. We were blessed by them all.

What also arrived, unwelcome yet fully present, was a sadness the strength and depth of which I had never experienced.

I was sad that this accident happened. Sad that I caused it. Sad that my husband had to experience the unimaginable pain of thinking I was dead at the scene and that he somehow was responsible for it. Sad for what my family experienced. Sad that I upset and worried my friends far and near. Sad that I had to stop working as a psychic medium, letting down all those who were counting on me for support during their time of grief. Sad that I stopped being me, and had stopped my normal life. Sad that I ruined my physical body, aging as it was, and that it will never be the same again. Sad that I had to be taken care of. Sad that I had to be hospitalized. Sad that I felt pain, weakness, and the inability to perform normal activities of daily living and personal care. Sad that I needed to rely on Craig and my family and friends to do even the most basic of things.

Deep, painful, scary sadness.

I cried, sobbed, multiple times a day for months. It was a most intense, remarkable experience. What was also intense and remarkable was that I surrendered to the experience, totally.

I remember the exact moment. It was my first night in the rehabilitation facility after being transported by EMTs. I was unsure of my surroundings. Unsure of the woman lying in the bed next to me (who turned out to be a wonderful roommate and a dear friend). Unsure of the nurse who did my intake, the staff, the facility, and whether or not I would receive my pain medication on time. My husband had left for home, exhausted and in much need of rest at 9 p.m.

I felt alone and afraid. I was on my own. I closed my eyes, took a deep breath, and I surrendered. With tears in my eyes and my heart wide open to receive, I asked the powers that be, the god of my understanding, my deceased father, my main spirit guide White Oak, my friends and family in spirit, angels, guides, and any energy of light who was willing, to surround me and protect me. I asked them to support me through the next part of this journey. I placed myself in their loving care, then I asked for guidance and strength, healing and understanding. I asked for the grace to accept what happened and for the strength to reclaim my life. I asked to be open to receiving help and to receive it with grace and gratitude. And I asked for peace. I drifted off to sleep feeling as if I was being held by a divine source more powerful than can be described here and surrounded once again in that beautiful soft light.

Don't misunderstand me, I was still suffering emotionally and physically, but after this experience of surrender, I felt better. There were months of physical and mental rehabilitative therapies, doctor visits, and pain modulation ahead of me, along with months and months of hard work to regain a normal semblance of life. But every single step along the way I was supported, encouraged, cared for, and loved. Delightful synchronicities and expressions of support, too many to mention, began to occur, and I was open to receiving it all. Because I surrendered and opened myself to becoming vulnerable and willing to receive, what I found was unconditional, unwavering love and support from my beautiful husband, who never once faltered or complained about his new set of "duties" surrounding my healing journey. Our connection grew stronger through this experience, and it remains strong today, after having been through it. I feel blessed beyond measure to have him in my life.

I was equally blessed by many others, my mother for example, who spent hours with me every day during the week I was in rehab and when I returned home as she "stood guard" over me, making sure I was resting and had everything I needed. I received the blessings of my siblings Susan, Rob, and Kelly, which included gifts to make me smile, crystals for healing, a special pillow case imprinted with my nephew Logan's healing hands, visits from New York, energy healings, raw turkey tips – a story for another day – and so much love. My dear brother-in-law Jim helped Craig return me home from the rehab center.

What was usually a one-minute sprint from the driveway to the house took them fifteen minutes. I enjoyed his visits with me during the months ahead. Craig's mother and father and families from Texas were a great support for us and we were blessed by their love.

I asked for help and support from a friend whose professional work was as a medical aide. She came to my home three times a week to help me with personal care. Lauren, my niece, arranged to visit from CA and supported me with love, and her brother Corey, my nephew, offered his support and love as wheelchair pusher, errand runner, constant visitor, and aide. I received with gratitude Patti Lou's company and her home-made chocolate chip cookies, as well as my friend Ellen's deep and meaningful conversations. I said yes to Ed and Jonathan's energy healing sessions, which they so generously offered. Friday became Paula day. She arrived every Friday for months with breakfast, lunch, and dinner for Craig and me. She was a constant comfort and along with making me take naps, and driving me to physical therapy until I could drive myself, she did laundry, too! Craig and I received every effort with gratitude. There were cards, notes, gifts, flowers, meals, books, poems, treats, texts, and prayers. There were messages, visits, energy sends, the largest bouquet of chocolate-covered fruit I ever have seen, and there was love, so much love. It was, at times, overwhelming, but, because I had surrendered, given up control, and allowed myself to be vulnerable, I was open to receiving.

I could sense the energy. I could feel it. I could feel the love, the prayers and the powerful loving thoughts. I know that each particle of energy created on my behalf, whether it was a thought, a prayer, or me being held in the light of healing, served a purpose, and I am grateful.

Deeply, profoundly grateful, even now.

At the time of this writing, almost six years have passed since that fateful day. The experience and all that surrounded it has woven itself into the fabric of my life as all experiences do and I have learned so much.

I learned that I am stronger than I thought I was. I guarantee that YOU are stronger than YOU think you are. **YOU ARE STRONG.**

I learned that it's okay to ask for help. It doesn't mean we are weak. Sometimes we just need some help. **ASK FOR HELP. RECEIVE IT WITH GRACE AND GRATITUDE.**

I realized just how important I am to the people in my life. **YOU ARE IMPORTANT TO THE PEOPLE IN YOUR LIFE. REALIZE IT.**

I have always been a strong and independent person. I learned that allowing myself to be vulnerable opened me to receive the love and support of the people around me and it's a beautiful thing. ALLOW YOURSELF TO BE VULNERABLE.

I learned that while it is hard at the time, adversity can strengthen relationships. ALLOW YOUR RELATIONSHIPS TO STRENGTHEN.

I learned that each blessing I received, no matter the size, carried the same energy of love and added to my healing experience. EXPRESS YOUR COMPASSION AND LOVE TO OTHERS, ALWAYS – ESPECIALLY IN TIMES OF NEED.

I learned that even though things happen around you and to you, it does not make you a victim. It's just something that happened. You can heal, you can work through it. CHOOSE TO HEAL.

I learned that if you have to press pause on your professional commitments, people will understand. PRESS PAUSE WHEN YOU NEED TO.

I learned to be gentle with myself. There are no expectations to live up to other than my own. I do not need to compare myself to anyone else's progress or non-progress. BE GENTLE WITH YOURSELF.

I learned that time really does heal. GIVE YOURSELF THE TIME YOU NEED. I did and I still am.

Mostly, I am well, but I am changed. I move more slowly, I can't do some of the things I used to physically, I need to pace myself or I will be reminded by my body to slow down. Gone are the days of the 1800-mile motorcycle trips I so enjoyed. However, I am here! I move at my own pace. I don't miss some of the things I can no longer do like raking leaves, shoveling snow, or lifting heavy things. Instead, I've learned to adapt and I do "other" things, and 1800-mile car trips can be just as fun!

What I also learned is that all is well, and from the experience I had and shared with my husband, my family and friends, only good has come. **ALL IS WELL.**

October 22nd, 2017. The day I could have died, but I didn't. Instead, I surrendered, I healed, and I learned.

After 27 years as a chiropractic physician, **Dr. Cathy Ripley Greene** retired from practice in June of 2017 to pursue her life-long love of healing through connections with Spirit. She is a gifted and sought-after psychic medium offering support to those with grieving hearts. Cathy is a force of positivity, generosity, and kindness. Her sessions are amazing, offering healing and understanding of the continuum of life. She believes we never truly die, we just become different and we reside in another dimension. Don't even get her started on quantum physics and the "dead peeps," unless you have some time because she loves to apply her knowledge of science to all things spiritual.

She resides south of Boston with her supportive, Virgo husband Craig Ripley, and a variety of people from spirit who move in and out of her life at will.

You can find out more about Cathy at: CathyRipleyGreene.com

Susan

SUSAN BRADWIN

WORDS OF WISDOM FROM A WIDOW

We all wish that it didn't happen, however, my husband passed away on July 23, 1997, after seven months of undergoing treatment for multiple myeloma. He had a successful bone marrow transplant, receiving the platelets from his sister Carolyn.

Scott also had an endoscopy. Unfortunately, they punctured his lung and he had to have a chest tube put in. He also developed graph versus host disease and then got pneumonia, which triggered multiple organ failure, ultimately resulting in his death. The following morning, I went out to my front porch and asked my late husband to be with me. I felt his hand on my right shoulder and heard, "I'm right here."

When I told my sister the story, she said, "He wouldn't have grabbed your shoulder, he would have grabbed your boobs!" Ha ha ha. Humor always helps us through difficult situations.

When I was about two years old, I pulled a very heavy shell

lamp down on my head by pulling on the cord in the living room. My parents had me on the kitchen table and applied pressure to my forehead. The bleeding finally stopped, but I have a nice scar there now. I remember being out of it for a while. It felt peaceful and dream-like to be comforted by the "angels." When I regained consciousness, I felt different, more connected, I suppose. I was concussed for quite a while. I remember my father Earle Torrey being very concerned about me.

I was also run over by Janice Turner on a bike when we went to the Whitman Town Park bike-decorating contest. It was the Fourth of July, and I was trampled. To this day, I always look for the exit in a crowd. I was six when I was taken to the hospital and checked out. I was fine. I felt "out of it" for a while. After this experience, I had premonitions – I often knew what people would say and do before they would do it. This was when I started to feel "different."

I had a total hysterectomy when I was 47. The doctor told me they had difficulty bringing me back from the anesthesia. I remember not wanting to come back. I spent time with my late husband in spirit and wanted to stay with him.

The night before the surgery, I could not sleep at all. I thought I was going to die during the operation. My late husband saved me, I know this. He sent me back to our three children and told me, "They still need you, and you aren't done yet. Go back. I will be here for you when it is your time and not a minute before. Go back."

We are all here for a reason. My reason, I believe, is to connect with loved ones in Spirit and to communicate messages from the angels and ascended masters. I'm also here to find the missing, or at least to locate them.

I am really looking forward to my reunion with my late husband Scott William Bradwin, my parents Earle and Miriam Torrey, all four of my brothers, my grandparents, my cousins, and my late daughter Amber Rose, to whom I dedicate this chapter in this book.

Jesus is my reiki guide. I have been in his presence many times. Mother Mary has also appeared to me as well. She guides me always. Archangel Michael is always with me when I drive, and my husband and late father are, too. If I could give any advice, I would tell people who have lost someone dear to them to give themselves time to heal.

"Feel it to heal it." Listen to music that you love. See the signs of your loved ones in spirit. Remember the good times and keep them close to you. Be with the memories if it makes you feel better. Take time to get to the place of accepting how things worked out.

There is a lesson in all of this, a love lesson.

Susan Bradwin aka Susie, is a psychic, angel medium, reiki practitioner, Akashic records reader, and table tipper. She comes from many generations of Irish descent with relatives who have also had these abilities as well, including her children and grandchildren.

Growing up, Susie thought everyone knew about her abilities and wasn't aware that other people did not have the same abilities. She does believe that we all have some, even if we don't recognize this. We can choose to develop them which she has done.

She has learned from some incredibly wise teachers, such as Maureen Hancock, Karen Paolino Correia, Teresa Lally, Jodi St. Onge, Debbie McBride, Radleigh Valentine, and Lynn Marie.

10

Lisa

LISA PONTE

FINDING MY VOICE

At 47 years old, I am finally ready to tell my story. It is one filled with pain, depression, and a life-changing suicide attempt. I am not sure exactly why I have kept this pain bottled up inside of myself for all of these years. Perhaps it was because of the fear of embarrassment, shame, being judged, or simply the idea of stirring up old feelings again. Back then, my family was conditioned to push feelings away and hide the truth. We all pretended as if everything was okay. Sharing my story has freed me from all those years of pain, suffering, and the time I spent cooped up in the prison of my own mind.

I was a popular cheerleader but had average grades. Sports and competition didn't seem to interest me. I had an older sibling, Tracy, two years older than me, and a younger brother Matthew, five years younger.

My story began in seventh grade when I started to get bullied. The bullies were a group of six older and more popular girls, aka the "Six Pack." The daily bullying was filled with vicious, vulgar, and abusive events that took place for the next dreadful five years. There are a few memories in particular that stick with me the most. One time I was walking up to my locker in between classes to grab my books when I heard loud footsteps behind me. My heart started to race as I heard the words, "You f'ing bit**, get out of my way!" The bullies continued to glare at me as I quickly grabbed my books and scurried off to my next class. I am sure others witnessed this abuse, but who was going to stop the most popular girls? I was profusely sweating and shaking uncontrollably as I tried to concentrate on my studies in class. Their name-calling only persisted and became more belligerent as the years went on. The girls followed me around every day, making my life miserable. It didn't matter where I was – football games, the locker room, parties – they always seemed to find me. Another memory that distinctly sticks with me was the time I was on a walk in my neighborhood – the same walk I frequently took after school to clear my sad thoughts – when I heard a car speeding up behind me. I turned around to see the six girls in a car swerving towards me. Each of them had their head hanging out of the window or sunroof laughing as they called me a "c*nt" at the top of their lungs. Not only could I not go to school in peace, but I also couldn't enjoy my time outside of school. I walked home with my heart full of anxiety and fear.

I am not sure why the bullying occurred, but I believe it had to do with their guy friend, who happened to be my boyfriend of five years. Our relationship was abusive and twisted. I had intercourse with him at thirteen years old, not really knowing what it was or how serious it was. He cheated, lied, and even fractured my arm, which I sadly covered up to protect him. I kept going back because I had no courage to leave. I wanted to fit in and feel loved, so I also experimented with alcohol and minor drugs to feel accepted.

He witnessed the bullying as did a few of my friends, but no adults knew, and certainly not anyone in my family.

Between the bullying, dysfunctional relationship and the struggle to fit in, I was feeling very down. I finally hit my low freshman year. Every time I tell this story, my eyes start to swell and my voice chokes up. I felt scared and lonely. I experienced the darkest day of my life and a parent's worst nightmare. I couldn't confide in my parents, siblings, or friends. My parents didn't communicate and express their feelings so it was difficult for me to confide in them. They didn't believe in intercourse before you were married, so I knew if I shared this information, they would be disgusted. I felt stuck and alone, and so isolated that I didn't want to live anymore. I decided to take my life. Today, you can google ways to kill yourself, but when I was younger, all I had was an encyclopedia. I really didn't know how to end my life, but I knew if I took enough pills, I could potentially die. I remember curling my hair and putting on a pretty pink blouse, then I walked out of my house for school with a bottle of pills. I sucked down over 30 pills, choking to get each one down. Almost immediately after my attempt, I was filled with feelings of regret and panic. I finally confided in a friend, who quickly notified a teacher. I was soon transported to the nearest hospital, where my stomach was pumped. My father sat next to me in the hospital bed as I watched tears roll down his face while I threw up black charcoal. My tears were flowing, my face red from embarrassment and my heart pounding.

After my attempt, I was kept in isolation for a few days and evaluated by a psychiatrist. I was eventually released and scheduled to start therapy, but it only lasted one session. My parents didn't believe in therapy, and they thought there were no other solutions except to confront the bully. My father advised my older sister to fight if words were exchanged at school. Of course, the next day, words were exchanged. My sister got into a physical altercation with the girl and was then suspended from school. I remember the principal calling my dad to tell him about the suspension, and he responded, "I gave her permission to fight," and the principal replied, "Off the record, she deserved to be hit." So although I eventually broke up with my boyfriend and graduated high school, I went off to college without ever really healing from my difficult experiences. I always questioned myself as to why I couldn't defend myself, why my self-confidence was low, and why I craved affection. My thoughts were in my head but never able to come out of my mouth. Where was my voice when I needed it? I think part of my low self-confidence and need to feel loved came from a situation I had with my father. My dad wasn't an overly affectionate man but we loved hanging out and watching TV together. As a little girl, he let me jump up on the couch and lay beside him, watching sports or the news. I loved having my dad wrap his arms around me and call me his Sheesh. One day he said, "You are too old for this sh*t," and told me to get the hell off. I felt extremely confused and sad. I imagine back in the day he didn't know how to deal with me getting older, and it made him uncomfortable. My father and I are extremely close today, but little did he know I struggled for any man to love me for years to come.

The bullying and abusive relationship stuck with me for the

next 20 years. I had no sense of love or respect for myself. I thought about suicide many times after but was so afraid of the consequences that I never attempted it again. My lack of confidence affected my friendships, career, and the thing that was dearest to my heart, my marriage. My husband and I had so many ups and downs that it eventually got to the point where I contemplated divorce. I felt like I was walking on eggshells trying not to make mistakes and upset him. I remember a time when I was visiting my parents in Florida. My flight got delayed and I needed him to pick me up at the airport at midnight. Now at the time, our children were younger, and it was a pain to pack them up, but I wasn't comfortable with a cab that late at night. All I could hear on the other end of the phone was screaming and rage. I felt like a child being scolded by her father. I didn't understand why these minor situations were so blown out of proportion. I was living a life filled with nerves and anxiety. We fought over everything and anything. One rainy and dreary day, I was walking out of Target, sobbing as I scurried to my car. I had finally hit rock bottom and couldn't take the fighting anymore. It was emotionally and physically draining, and I felt defeated, knowing that if something didn't change, I would have to live the rest of my life feeling this way.

My husband and I decided to stick together, but we both knew major changes needed to be made, including lots of counseling and communication. Throughout this process, I developed a strong sense of self-worth. Our marriage was eventually pieced back together. Steve worked hard on his rage by meditating, changing jobs, and working on his response to situations. He promised he would never go back to that version of himself, and he didn't. My therapist said 90% of people cannot change their behaviors or patterns, but our marriage and family meant the world to him. I was no longer afraid to use my voice, and the fear and anxiety in our relationship subsided. I realized that I deserved happiness, and the only one who could make me happy was me. This rough patch in my marriage taught me how to love myself for all that I am, the good and the bad. It taught me what I would and would not tolerate. I became independent during this difficult time in my marriage and started my own spiritual journey of healing. I knew there was a path to happiness and I would find it. I took the time to reflect within. I participated in a 40-day personal revolution class where I practiced meditation and yoga every day, which led me to my love for yoga. I then decided to obtain my 200-hour Yoga Teacher Training (YTT). I started spending quiet time with myself and my thoughts. I worked through different yoga poses that released pain and stuck emotions.

My mother-in-law, Paulette, who I love, lived with us for five years and witnessed the toughest years of our marriage. She was my sounding board and my friend. During this hard time, she gifted me a set of affirmation cards. When I received them, I had no idea what they were: little did I know, they would forever change my life. This unexpected act of kindness and sweet gesture from my mother-in-law was the jumpstart into my lifelong journey of self-love. From this point on, I made it my mission to rediscover the love and happiness for myself that I deserved, and affirmation cards became a key tool to my achievement of this goal. I started pulling a positive card each morning.

In 2020, when the Covid-19 pandemic hit, I looked around and saw many anxious and scared individuals. They reminded me of my old self. I wanted to be able to form meaningful connections and help others because I knew what it was to feel surrounded by darkness. I decided to start my very first company, LP Vibes. It started with creating my own deck of affirmation cards. My mission was to spread positivity and happiness into people's lives one card at a time. I wanted to be a light in people's lives and a support system for individuals who were going through difficult times and didn't have anyone to lean on.

My words have been the motivation that some individuals lost, the support others were striving to find, and the love that everyone deserves. My favorite part of this journey has been touching the lives of others. I have been able to help people stay positive during times of depression, divorce, illness, and death. If I spent my days waiting for the perfect time to launch my business, then this deck of cards would not exist. Instead, I combated my fears head-on. My business is only just beginning, and I can't wait to see where it goes and how many more lives I am able to touch.

To end, I will leave you with the message from the affirmation card that I selected today: "Mistakes are okay, emotions are okay, regrets are okay. Be gentle on yourself, after all, you are human." I hope sharing my story gives you the strength to find your inner voice. We all need to be heard.

Lisa Ponte is the founder of the company LP Vibes. She lives in Westwood, MA with her husband Steve, two daughters (Alex and Kya), and three pups (Mugsy, Moose, and Manny). She picks an affirmation card and practices gratitude on a daily basis. She lives by her mantra, "Rise & Reset Your Mind." What you are reading today, she shares with courage, confidence, and without any shame. After all, she is human.

To learn more about LP Vibes please visit: www.lpvibes.com

11

Pavlina

PAVLINA GATIKOVA

THE SOURCE WITHIN THE SELF

"*Each of us has a unique purpose and path. The details of our lives may differ, but our mission remains the same: to move closer to love.*" — Dr. Judith Orloff

"*Rarely, if ever, any of us healed in isolation. Healing is an act of communion.*" — Bell Hooks

A twenty-five-year-old me got it in my head that it was in the United States of America where I would find love. My fortune teller predicted that I would meet him there, and he'll be a bit older than me. At that time I didn't factor the age in, no problem, so what if he's a bit older? I saw him in my dreams, too, so it has to be true, right?

I will be loved there, not here in the Czech Republic.

This place is lost on me. Nothing good can come out of my staying here, I believed. That I was sure of, and I was determined to travel throughout the country to find that right person for me. Did I really know what I wanted? Vaguely. Mostly no, though. I created a list of qualities I wanted in a partner, but they all seemed to be a bit conditioned by societal expectations. Finding love outside myself was my mission, I had no concept of self-love, self-worth, self-acceptance, or what truly was inside of me. I was too frightened to look and see all of myself then. I was so hyper-focused on my fears, feeling ashamed of them and my angst and insecurities. I didn't realize that all of us have all of these in some shape and form, yet I just wasn't ready to accept them. They were to be banished, as they were stopping me from feeling okay, or at least good enough.

Through my parents, I witnessed how the male partner berated and negated the woman, how he always had to be a step higher than her. How her truths, no matter how outrageous they may have seemed to him, are equally as valid as his. There was no reciprocity or equal share of power in their relationship. I detested that, even though I adored my father as a child and I was on his side then. I thought my mother was in the wrong for being a Communist and my father being right as a new Democrat. I thought he deserved to be loved, and I forgot that my Mother was equally deserving of his love, too. I wanted her to accept him, to love him as hard, as unconditionally, as blindly as I did, as children are wired to do. I wanted her to take my place, because deep down I did not want to play the role of an emotional wife. I may have been proud then to be so proficient and praised by him for it, but deep down, I resented my place. I wanted to be loved as a child, to be given love as a child.

BEGINNINGS:

A girl was born in the Jeseniky Mountains, on December 7th,

1974, to a young couple of Communist idealists who believed they could create a better world. She was born into the cold. It was winter, snow on the ground. She was most likely separated from her mother at birth, which caused her great distress. She was born to a couple who was not quite ready for her arrival. They were both just trying to survive, separate maybe from the family of origin, finding safety in an ideology, as my mother could not feel safe with her violent and alcoholic father. My father was also righting some kind of wrong. He wrote poetry, too. The new family didn't have a place to live, so they got some help from relatives. They had to get married, as they got pregnant. My mother was still in college. Her daughter was born before she was able to graduate, and she never had a chance to go back, as she wanted her husband to complete his law degree. He went to night school in order to become a lawyer, and she took care of her daughter. My father was an alcoholic whom my mother thought she would be able to reform.

I never saw my father drunk until one night when I was about ten or twelve. Seeing my father in such a compromised state made me wonder about his hero status. Something shifted for me then. He no longer was the perfect dad. Deep down, I got to see a glimpse of his darker sides. Unfortunately, my younger self couldn't bear that type of vision of her father, so she buried this memory deep down. This God all of a sudden stumbles and is out of control, not as strong as my child self wanted and needed him to be. My younger self so wanted to hold onto the image of her dad as a superhero, someone who always has an answer to a question even if it is completely made up, someone who can spin a funny and outrageous story in no time, someone who can make me belly laugh, someone who plays with me and my siblings when he's finally home from a long day at work. But he chose to either go drinking with his buddies or stay at work to avoid the wife he was not emotionally connected to.

My mother was the one who was always there physically for us. She was not an affectionate mother, and did not know how to show us that she loved us. It was a given that she loved us, but we were never shown the extent of her love. She would make sure we were taken care of, then my father just came home late and we would flock to him as if he was the second coming of Christ. We wanted him, not our mother. We provided the captivating audience for him that he badly needed. I never acknowledged as a child how much my mother endured with her husband, who on the outside looked like a caring, hard-working husband, but behind the walls of our apartment, he could turn pedantic, giving her the silent treatment if she didn't go along with what he wanted.

Twenty-three years ago, on January 7th or so, I landed at the T.F. Green International Airport in Providence, RI to spend a year as an au pair in the United States. I was twenty-five years old, laid off from my job as a high school teacher of English and French as a foreign language, and newly single after a long-term relationship with a man 10-years my senior. I fell in love with him at the age of 17. I had no clue about how to express myself emotionally in this first relationship. So, I hid behind the intellectual and spiritual interests I shared with my boyfriend. We were both seekers on a path toward enlightenment through Zen meditation. I believed meditation was all about stopping all my thinking and finding, bliss in a place of quiet and excluding my desires and emotions. It worked. I was hurting (completely unaware of how much) and spiritual bliss was my way to salvation. It anesthetized me from all my negative feelings and sensations. It could not have been that bad, as my more experienced, more mature boyfriend was looking for the same. The term for this type of coping mechanism. is a spiritual bypass. Instead of facing difficult feelings or unresolved issues, you rationalize them with spiritual explanations.

In 1999, I broke off with my boyfriend ungracefully in the Czech Republic. Part of me is ashamed that I had to cheat on him to break away. I could not just say *no, I no longer want to be with you.* Again, looking at it from a trauma perspective or my conditioning, I was unable to say no to men. That was dangerous. That was not acceptable, unheard of. I was determined to step away from the life I had lived in the Czech Republic. I was so looking for a clean slate, a fresh start, so to speak. All of me wanted badly to abandon the Czech me and embrace the free spirit of my American self, the free self, the expressive self, the creative self. I wanted to put a stop to the "self" that was so perfect at following the rules, being the good girl, keeping my mouth shut, not wanting anything, not having any needs, doing what was right for the family, being a dutiful and loyal daughter. It no longer fit me. I wanted to shed that robe of repression of what was naturally inside me that I really had no connection to.

Part of me was desperate to find love outside of myself. Another part knew her lover was here, somewhere in this large country. I had no idea where, but I was determined to keep looking till I bumped into him. And I did, at the College Hill Bookstore in Providence on May 6, 2000. He was the stranger I accepted the ride from as I refused to pay a third of my au pair salary for a taxi. I put in it in my head that someone would bring me home for free. This man, who looked like he could be my grandfather, as his hair was gray, was willing to. I trusted him. He could have been a serial killer, but at that time I had no self-preservation instincts, so I accepted the ride to my home in East Greenwich, RI, where I lived with my host family. The best mistake of my life could have been the worst and cost me my life, but it wasn't. It was the most right thing I did.

Alan has been a refuge to me. When I first came here, I was feeling so depleted, out of place, feeling so unlovable, yet I wanted love so badly. I was so hungry for it. Though I thought of myself as undeserving. Who would ever want to love me? The unloveable part of me was occupying a very large portion of myself, so she'd go for any kind of loving. Fortunately, my husband is capable of being in a healthy relationship and being affectionate. When I went into it, I was not. I needed receiving, being nurtured into deserving physical touch, being told sweet things and allowing them to reach me, and receiving the pleasure of physical intimacy without shame. I have never met a man before who wanted to make me happy. My first boyfriend did not do that. I didn't know that was part of a relationship to make each other happy and not at the expense of each other's well-being.

I am still married to this man, happily, and grateful for what he has taught me about loving relationships and how they can work. At home in the Czech Republic, I saw mostly how painful being in a relationship can be.

At first, I was intent on looking for love outside of myself. That lasted up until I felt really safe in the relationship with my husband. Once that sense of safety was established, I became comfortable exploring my internal existence. I moved away from trying to fuse with him and wanted to find out what I liked on my own. About 10 years ago, I began to journal to explore my inner world. I began to focus on myself: my feelings, desires, and interests as opposed to what I was conditioned to focus on, which was mainly accommodating, serving, and pleasing others.

In addition to journaling, I was determined to write my own memoir, but I didn't get to do that. Halfway through, I got stuck on my lack of perspective, and lack of distance from my past and my childhood upbringing. In addition, I was really pulled toward writing poetry. This seemed to be my way to go. I found that I feel very comfortable in the skin of a poet in love with words, the sensual aspect of poem writing, the density of expression, and mostly the emotional impact the poems can have on their audience. I want to always connect with my reader's emotions and deeper truths that are not able to be tapped into through our own minds.

However, the journey to trusting myself as a poet was not an easy one. I could not just sit down and write a poem. I had to find myself a mentor, as I was totally lacking in the department of trusting that I could pull it off. In time, I began to trust, but it still can be a big chore to overcome my own negative conditioning and my critical parts and need to control the creative process. As I get older, I am learning to lean into the process more versus being right and not making any mistakes. Perfectionism is something I am practicing to acknowledge more and be more compassionate by using this as a survival strategy which served me well in my childhood but does not support me now in my adulthood. Yet, I believe now I am more or less ready to embrace my imperfect self a little more and allow myself to make mistakes just for the sake of messing up and learning something from them. Failure is only a failure if I take it as such. It all depends on what perspective I take in regard to my errors.

The writing, expressly the practice of morning pages, led me to yoga, namely Kripalu yoga, in other words, the yoga of compassion. Let me tell you, being self-compassionate is something I am still inching towards. There is so much I still do not fully embrace about myself. Yet, I am learning to recognize that even that is a process. I even got certified and taught as a volunteer in a library for a while. Again, my negative patterning and the fact that yoga connects you to your body had me stop for a while, as powerful emotions kept resurfacing. I had no idea how to deal with them; therefore, I paused with practice.

Fast forward to 2019, my pivotal year, as it was during this year that a writer friend of mine recommended I enter IFS therapy, as I was looking for a way to improve my relationship with my father. Little did I know that an IFS therapeutic model is really not a strategy-based tool, it is a therapeutic model that invites you in. You focus on yourself, namely components of yourself, which they call parts. The IFS model has a spiritual component as well, which I was also attracted to. The higher self, in IFS, represents qualities such as compassion, connection, calm, perspective, presence, patience, etc. Surprisingly, connecting to my parts and self came very easily to me and I was experiencing discoveries about myself, even connecting the larger aspect of myself that connects me to my essence. I was elated and liberated. Parts of me wanted relief from the feelings of deep disconnect, invisibility, low self-esteem, self-doubt, and the exorbitant need to be validated and seen.

So this was the year I began my emotional literacy training. I did not know what I was getting myself into. Luckily, I had a wonderful therapist and an IFS-informed friend with whom we spent Saturday mornings exploring our parts and exiles. This time with my Slovak friend Lenka taught me about the intricacies of complex trauma, developmental trauma, and emotional neglect, which I have been deeply impacted by for most of my life without even realizing it. In addition, as I deepened my connection to my parts, flashbacks began to appear, alerting my body that it had been betrayed. This was a very disturbing realization for me, and even though I am friends with a friend who experienced sexual abuse, I myself didn't want to acknowledge any of that. I had all the "right" feelings pointing to the fact that someone must have taken advantage of my little body, but I had no recollection of anything. In my writing, I wrote extensively about my father and how my relationship with him was very sexual in nature, but I attributed that to my being his emotional wife. It wasn't until recently that a memory resurfaced that he touched me inappropriately when I was about five years old. I still am not sure how to deal with this, but I feel empowered and liberated by the truth experiencing the rage of that five-year-old being deeply betrayed by someone who was supposed to protect her, which I was not able to see until now. No wonder I was so distrusting of men and felt unprotected around them. A close connection to a trusted male friend helped me uncover this deep distrust of men. At last, I am beginning to release the rage and embody joy and freedom of sexual expression instead.

Acknowledging how deeply I felt unseen in the family of origin where there was no room to express emotions unless you were a father, meant entering a long period of ongoing grief of what was lost within me and buried under the abundant rug of "feelings are not to be seen, needs are not to be expressed, discontent is supposed to stay in, not be voiced, anger's forbidden, my needs are not legitimate, girls can only say yes, no is not in their dictionary." The more I felt invisible at home, the more I withdrew inward into the world of books and imagination, where everything was possible, love was attainable and given in a healthy way, relationships were reciprocal, boundaries were clear, members of the family were seen for who they were, and there was safety in expressing oneself freely. That is where I felt free from harm — in my head and holding onto a book. The world of language and knowledge was my safe haven. Attending to my body and its cues felt hazardous; hence I avoided going there.

As a wounded healer, my commitment is to deepening the relationships to my parts and creating an inclusive community of them within. If I can heal my own system with the support of the right individuals and facilitate harmonious interactions among my parts, I can certainly be able to provide the same for others. However, the work of the wounded healer begins with me, with my commitment to continuous growth and healing. The aspiration to support the healing of others comes as a natural outflow of having addressed my own traumatic history and recognition that a better world begins with a healed and whole individual, which is me. I deeply believe that healing needs to take place in a community or within a safe space with safe individuals. My goal is to create and cultivate those spaces where one by one, we can come to our own wholeness through the power of our interconnectedness.

Pavlina Gatikova relocated from the Czech Republic to the United States in 2000, representing the first step towards her personal growth. She is a seeker and wounded healer committed to her own journey through the Internal Family Systems (IFS) model, also known as Parts Work, from which she experienced deep transformation and continues to do so. Pavlina finds this modality deeply resonant and life-changing, and she would like to support others on their paths to self-discovery and transformation. She completed level One IFS training in May 2021. Prior to the discovery of IFS, she used writing, namely journaling, to support her own healing and healing of others. She has been facilitating women's journaling at the Attleboro Public Library since 2018. She is a certified Kripalu yoga instructor, poet, and avid journaler.

12

Courtney

COURTNEY RICCI

WOUNDS TO WISDOM

PART 1:

I never really had a place I called home. I was born in Massachusetts but turned 18 in a state far from here. I was a high school varsity cheerleader. No pets, and no siblings that ever lived at home. It was a pretty quiet and lonely life. My adoptive mother had untreated mental illness and addiction issues. She worked nights and stayed busy with other things, so she was never around much. It had been that way since the divorce back in middle school, moving someplace new every year of high school – a new school, new people, new state, new life. We moved there in August just in time for my junior year of high school to begin. A few weeks after my 18th birthday in December, she packed up all her things on a whim and left. She decided North Carolina was the place to be, so off she went. Lucky for me, my stuff was still there.

I moved to a homeless shelter in the nearest city and got back into school to finish my junior year. A few months later, I dropped out and enrolled in night school. I started dyeing my hair bright rainbow colors, wore heavy black eyeliner, and looked like something out of Hot Topic. I was able to secure myself a room in a transitional living program until I moved in with my boyfriend at the time. We were 18 and meant well. He played bass in a band, I worked as a florist at the local grocery store. Things fizzled out between us in under a year, and I moved back to the city with a friend I knew who always let people crash at her place. Though I had applied for local jobs everywhere I could find, I never got hired. Instead, I thrived on being popular and well-liked. There was always a party going on somewhere. That's how I met Page one day at a house party. She was my age, tall, with rainbow top hair, and had a car, money, drugs, and a badass attitude. We quickly became best friends. I didn't know it at the time, but that girl was going to teach me better life lessons than any parent I've ever met. But they were different kinds of life lessons. The kind you only gain from experience.

Though my mother growing up was an addict, I managed to stay on the straight and narrow up until she ditched me. Maybe a little weed here and there, but that's nothing. It was actually Page who introduced me to the wonderful world of drugs, and the very interesting people who lived in it. Being young and carefree, I thought of it as nothing more than buying a bag of feelings, and I assumed everyone else did too. Harmless fun, really. People looked like they had so many friends and were having so much fun, and I wanted to be a part of that. So down the rabbit hole we went.

The great thing about Page was she had a house in the woods where I could practically live with her in between our adventures. There were no rules, no consequences, no issues...or so I thought.

The glory days didn't last long. Fast forward a year, and the scene began to look a lot different. For everyone around me, those harmless bags of fun turned into absolute necessities to get through a simple day. I couldn't understand it. Page and everyone else around me could not live without it. Everyday. It got so bad that I even watched Page shoot up into an infection in her arm. They would get physically ill without it, but I never had that problem. I was fine just smoking a little weed the day after doing any hard narcotic. It was around that time when I began to truly understand the power of addiction and the tight reigns it held on most people.

By the time I turned 20, most of my friends had either overdosed and died, gone to jail, or were in a seriously bad place. I had watched several people overdose in front of me, and at the same time, I saw the entire house full of people flee the scene instead of calling for help. I had involved myself with obnoxious criminals who preyed on completely innocent people for the sole purpose of getting more drugs. Frankly, I really hated who I was becoming. I took a break from the drugs while some friends were away. Once the fog in my brain cleared for a second, I took a leap of faith and reached out to an old friend from my freshman year of high school in Massachusetts.

He surprisingly and extremely willingly moved me to his house not far from where I reside now, with his family, and I was able to get a full-time job at the local Dunkin Donuts. Things were going well until he decided to go on his own secret narcotic binger and crash his truck at 3 a.m., a stunt that landed him in rehab for a few months. I used the money from my Dunks job to rent my very own first apartment conveniently down the street from my work. And though at just 20 years old, as I moved the minimal belongings I had left to my name into that big, white, empty apartment, I couldn't help but feel like I had finally, at least just for that moment, found my way home. And it was mine. Nobody else's, just mine.

PART 2:

I had just turned 21. I had my own place but with an awful roommate, two full-time jobs, and a handful of local friends, including my best friend Bree from freshman year of high school, who I re-connected with. We are still close today.

I also had a deepening depression growing every day. I ate extremely little because I could not afford to eat and pay my portion of the growing rent, which was not even close to being evenly split. But I didn't learn healthy boundaries until later on in my 20s. I woke up every day to get to work at the local elderly home at 6 a.m. and leave at 2 p.m. Then I would go to the local bar down the street to work from 3 p.m. – 10 p.m. or midnight every night. Mondays were my days off, and I usually spent them in bed in my room with my ferret, Marley. I was running myself dry every day and had nothing to show for it. When was life supposed to get easier?

Eventually, through friends, I met a local guy who became my boyfriend. I moved in with him and his buddies down the road. I began the process of going back to my natural hair color and began to really tone down my makeup and clothing style. I quit both of my jobs and found a better job as a floral designer once more, working for a woman who owned a flow-er shop close to where I lived. I also got to live there rent-free in exchange for taking care of the house and the three cats and dog that were left behind while John, the homeowner, traveled the world with our roommates for nine to ten months out of the year. I got two more ferrets, and life was beginning to look a little brighter.

It was during this time that I was awakened at 4 a.m. by a series of dings going off on my phone from a random woman I did not know. I read the very lengthy messages she was sending me and realized it was my biological little sister from my dad's side. She had spent years trying to find me. She was in high school and lived in Massachusetts, not too far away.

I learned that my dad's side of the family was from the Azores, and he was only 17 when I was born. My boss at the floral shop let us meet there for the first time. She took photos and was so happy for us. My sister and I are closer now and we talk often. However, when we went to visit our dad for the first time together, I noticed some red flags that she was too young to really understand, particularly relating to drug abuse. Our father is not actively involved in either of our lives now. That's okay with me. I can't really miss someone who was never really around to begin with. But it was nice meeting my three little brothers. I have enjoyed watching them grow up via social media from afar.

Things were really nice until we got the call one day in late April. John had crashed his vehicle and two of our roommates had died. His dog Kina was lost wandering the desert, and John was in the hospital in Colorado. I used my intuition and connections to find Kina a few days later. My boyfriend took the next flight out after I located the dog. He went to get her in Colorado and see John in the hospital. My boyfriend never came back though. John needed a traveling companion, and apparently an offer my boyfriend simply could not refuse came up. He ended up staying out West with John and the cats and another pup.

I had luckily made more friends in the community and had been hanging out with my current boyfriend of over five years. I moved to the Boston area, where I reside now with him. We got three more ferrets, and he came with a pup, all happy and healthy as I write this today. We originally worked growing cannabis together, but found he could make more money as a licensed plumber.

I was still battling depression. Some days I wouldn't get out of bed if I didn't have to. It wasn't until I finally decided to take the first step in what turned out to be my self-healing journey, that I began to truly change for the best.

PART 3:

It all started at Chill in Walpole, when I decided I couldn't take the constant discomfort anymore and booked myself a massage one night. The lady was kind and we got to talking, and she asked me if I wanted to go to this party just up the street with her after the massage because she was scared to go alone. I said, "Sure! Why not, right?" We ended up at this magical place called WeBreathe Wellness on the night of their fifth-anniversary party. I had no clue what a wellness center was or who the people inside were. But, I knew they looked like the kind of women I always wanted to be, but could never quite figure out how to become. You know, all happy, married, successful, shiny, well-dressed, and popular. It's like the women there had found some secret key to life success or something. They all seemed truly happy, and happy to be there. A few of them even talked to me! Me, in my black yoga pants and bleach-stained sweatshirt with massage oil in my hair and no makeup. And they were talking, very kindly I might add, to me! I couldn't believe it. I ended up joining the collaborative membership that they offered there that week and started showing up. I was 27 at the time.

It gave me a reason to get out of bed, it gave me a reason to dress up again and try. It was there at this wellness center that I first began to process and really acknowledge my biological mother Rose's death. She died of fentanyl in March 2020, and I never took the time to address it because I honestly did not know how to. So I just buried myself in my work and in my bed. I soon got my first reiki session done by the owner Jenn, and it was quite a heavy experience. That was my body's first introduction to energy work. I didn't have a key logical reason to keep showing up, but something kept calling me back to the center.

I began to take classes on sacred geometry and Akashic Records reading. I had my first mediumship experience there at a sampling event, and Rose came through with details no one could possibly know, as she never had any social media profiles, moved around a lot, and was pretty low-key. My cousin even went to see the same medium, Cathy R. Greene, last year and had an amazing experience of her own.

I had accomplished my goal of becoming a certified mediator during the Covid crisis. So, that and my cannabis experience did get me an opportunity to begin teaching classes at the wellness center on clean cannabis and healthy communication skills. And so, a teacher was born. I had always liked learning new things and teaching others how to accomplish a greater sense of self. So it felt like the right fit for me, to write and teach my classes. Some were more popular than others, but that's all part of the experience. I learned to not take failure personally and to look at how I could make changes to have a better outcome next class instead.

On the night of the Aries new moon in April 2022, a woman by the name of Maureen Hancock came to the wellness center to do one of her monthly mediumship events. We Breathe was short-staffed that night, so they called me up to see if I could help set up and go to the event for free. After the show, Maureen pulled me into a back office and asked me if I knew I was intuitively gifted and unique. I shrugged and said "I don't know.". She then gave me a free scholarship to her university for intuitively gifted individuals for life! I began to learn how to use my intuitive gifts in different ways and learn about the chakras, the human body, clearing mental clutter, using the Akashic Library and mediumship to help locate missing persons (a specialty of Maureen's), and much more. I even performed my first accurate live mediumship at Maureen's "Soul Shift" Retreat in Walpole MA on November 29, 2022!

I got inspired and put myself through a year-long herbal medicine program with one of the collaborative members, Jess, who is a practicing herbalist. She taught me the wonders of intuitive tea tastings, which is when you make tea out of one specific herb without knowing anything about the herb itself. Then you sip the tea and notice little things like if the energy expands or shrinks. Where is it storing and going inside of you? Then see if any medicinal effects come up in your intuitive hits. Then we go over all the textbook medical risks and benefits of each herb we study. I'll be finishing that program in September of 2023.

In 2022, I was reunited with my biological mother Rose's side of the family for a funeral in MA. We still all talk to this day, and I spent last Christmas and Fourth of July with them for the first time in a very long time. I learned that my great-grandmother Helen came over on a boat from England with my grandmother Mary, when she was two. I have two more siblings on my mother's side as well, an older brother and younger sister. I talk to both of my sisters pretty often. I have also particularly loved getting to know all my cousins on both sides and all the rest of both families. However, I will admit I do wish I was there for all the great memories and stories that they all still talk about to this day. That part still makes me sad. I really hope to be included in the making of more great family memories in the future.

On a personal level since then, I have created the tri-part Ophiuchus Medical Oracle Deck and my Death Speaks Oracle Deck. Both have no replicas. I have gained great confidence in the art of reading Oracle cards. I read the Akashic records, and I have helped find missing people intuitively. I am now Reiki two certified, and created/ teach an entry-level "Getting to Know Your Chakras" class that inspires others to be their best selves. I also created and teach the "Educating the Everyday Cannabis Consumer" class to help educate the community on many different aspects of cannabis from how it reacts within our bodies, to clean vs. toxic growing practices, and much more.

As I write this now at 29 years old, I have begun the lifelong journey of healing my chakras, soul, body, mind, and Spirit. Because of this, I now find myself in a place where I can truly say I know who I am, and I love myself with confidence. My hair, along with everything else on me, is all-natural. I feel beautiful in my own skin and have my own unique style. I have made a small business out of my intuitive skills and joined three different local networking groups to help get myself out there. I have money saved, and we are planning vacations. I finally became that kind of woman. Like the ones I saw on my first night at the center.

So the lessons are these. You can accomplish anything realistic that you set your mind to, and magic is real. The more you believe in it, the more it believes in you. Embrace your Spiritual self. Do the next right thing, and trust your instincts and intuition, especially when a person or situation does not feel right. There is a reason it does not feel right, so listen to that voice deep within that really wants to see you win. Don't forget to show up. Show up for a friend, and show up for yourself. Always be humble, graceful, and grateful, especially when receiving personal wins in your life. But I think the most important lesson of all that I learned in my twenties is that no matter where you go or end up in this life, you can choose to make a home or sanctuary with a great support system around you, if you allow yourself to do so. So let yourself be happy, I say. Let yourself give and receive LOVE. Let yourself be home, because YOU make it so.

Courtney Ricci is a 29-year-old local to the Gillette Stadium area. She is an experienced high-quality cannabis grower and educator, and teaches a class she created, "Educating the Everyday Cannabis Consumer." She is the co-owner and creator of Herbal Elixirs, a customizable mocktail party/ event pop-up. Additionally, she is the owner of Courtney Ricci Healing and specializes in reading the Akashic Records and Oracle cards. She uses the Akashic Library to study different diseases and cures and find missing people. She created the one-of-a-kind Ophiuchus Medical Oracle Deck and the Death Speaks Oracle Deck. Lastly, she is a Reiki healer and chakra educator who created and teaches her "Getting to Know Your Chakras" class, designed for those looking for an introduction to spirituality.

To get to where she is today, Courtney overcame many obstacles in her life and hopes that this story will inspire and motivate others to leave behind what no longer serves them.

You can reach Courtney on Instagram: @CourtneyRicci1321 or @HerbalElixirsMA

JESSICA LAMONTAGNE

LOVE YOURSELF SO OTHERS CAN, TOO

Growing up I always felt like a big fish in a small pond. I graduated in a class of less than 160 people and, I was a talented athlete and a gifted student. I was confident, outgoing, charismatic, friendly, and level-headed — a leader who was optimistic about the future.

I met "Jose" in 2003 when I was 15 years old. He told me he was 18. We worked in the same building. He was from Latin America, and I was intrigued by his interest in me. After he chased me for a few weeks, I gave in and gave him my phone number. We spent time together after work some days and that was the most it ever was, and it lasted around a year. To me, it felt like he was "obsessed" with me in a good way. I felt like I had the upper hand in the relationship and I liked it that way.

I graduated high school in 2006 and went off to college in a neighboring state. Now I felt like a minnow in the depths of the ocean. To say my confidence was shaken is an under-statement. I felt my life spiraling socially and academically. These people came from money, and I didn't. I had to work at the University's post office – how embarrassing. None of my college friends needed to work because they had their parents' credit cards. It seemed like everyone was going out during the week but me – I had to study and had no money. I had to work hard to keep up with my grades – I wasn't used to that. It was a true wake-up call. After a few failed attempts at a relationship and gaining the "freshman 15", my confidence and self-esteem were at an all-time low. I needed something that was safe – a sure thing.

During my sophomore year of college, I reached out to Jose because I needed to feel wanted. And for a while, it was great. I felt confident again. I was pregnant less than a year later. On June 9, 2009, I gave birth to our daughter. Then, the first red flag appeared. I was still in the hospital and was filling out our daughter's newborn paperwork. That's when he told me he was not, in fact, three years older than me, but he was actually six years older.

During the first few years of our daughter's life, I noticed a change in our relationship. I tried to connect with him as much as possible. I tried to communicate how I was feeling, that he had changed. He was not affectionate or caring, and I felt as though he was indifferent in our relationship and he didn't find me attractive anymore. Our phone calls wouldn't last more than two minutes. He never wanted to talk to me about anything, and it seemed like we had nothing in common. He wouldn't let me go near his phone and, he wouldn't tell me his passcode and claimed it was "private" (red flag #2). I never understood this. How could two people have children together and have secrets from one another? This never sat right with me. I knew he was hiding things, I just didn't know to what extreme. I had built up some resentment because we did not live together or share parenting duties until our daughter turned two. She looked at him like he was a stranger, you know, the way little kids are scared to talk to, go near, or interact with strangers. There were lots of ups and downs, and many times I tried to break it off but was scared of being a young, single mom still living with my parents. I saw no way out that wouldn't leave me single and living with my parents forever. I tried to make it work.

We got married on April 9, 2012. He was not a citizen and had come to this country illegally. I felt that to give our daughter the best life with the most opportunities, he had to have access to those same opportunities. After two years and approximately $15,000, he became a permanent resident.

In February 2015, our beautiful son came into this world. He was the happiest baby. Our relationship was on and off, "rocky" at best. But I dealt with it because my kids kept me happy and I focused on them. I still felt that he was not particularly attracted to me. We barely spent any time together, and we were drifting apart.

It was in July of 2015 that my life got flipped upside down. I found out he had been having an affair with a woman he worked with for three years. I had pictures, location history, and the woman's admission, but he denied everything. His entire family knew about the affair and were friends with this girl. My body broke down. I knew it. I had felt it in my body but ignored all the signs. Everything went through my brain. I had a small baby, another child in school, and no job. We hadn't been happy for a long time. He cringed whenever I would lean in to kiss him. I felt unloved and alone most of the time. What would I do? Move back in with my parents with two children and no job? I would never be able to survive on my own if I stayed in our condo alone. I felt ashamed, embarrassed, and sick to my stomach. I physically could not stomach the thought of food. I dropped about 30 lbs. in a month. My family was concerned, but whenever they tried to reach out, I hermitted. I didn't want anyone to know what was going on. I couldn't eat or sleep. Every time I tried to break it off, he would cry at my feet and beg me not to leave, yet he wouldn't stop lying and hiding things. He changed the passcode on his phone daily, he would download texting apps so that I couldn't trace his texts or calls, and he gaslit me at every accusation. I was "crazy," "always looking to fight," and "annoying." He promised me he would stop talking to her and begged for another chance. So I caved.

This went on for a year. Every time I thought he was telling me the truth and would stop seeing this girl, she would reach out to let me know that they were still together. I filed for divorce. He guilted me into rescinding because of his green card situation. I'm not sure when they actually ended things, but was like we swept everything under the rug and just moved on. Things would be okay for a few months, then go back to the same old routine of him ignoring me, changing his passcode, hiding things, and me feeling lonely.

In late 2018, the same exact scenario played out again. This time he was at a different job and it was with another coworker of his. The same storyline was repeating. I was sick to my stomach again. Why? How? What is the point of staying with someone if you're so unhappy that you cheat on them? I didn't understand. I felt like I wasted my life on this man, and I wasn't even happy! Again I said I wanted a divorce, he cried at my feet begging me to stay with him. I filed for divorce. I have never been more scared in my entire life. I accepted the fact that I would most likely have to move back in with my parents. But I went through with it. I accepted the fact that I might not meet a man who would accept me, my children, and my baggage. In October of 2019, I was officially divorced.

I was scared, lonely, and felt like I would be alone forever. During this time, I daydreamed a lot about life with someone who checked all my boxes. I compiled a list in my head without even realizing it. I made note of people's relationships around me and things that made me smile about those relationships. There were even things on my list that stemmed from childhood memories.

By March of 2020, I was officially living alone with my two kids trying to figure out how I would afford to stay in the condo I was living in. Then, Covid happened. I didn't realize it at the time, but the Universe was helping me. I was given the funds to be able to stay where I was living and continue the lifestyle my children were used to. Then, my daughter was diagnosed with the virus at the beginning of April. I was really alone now. Me and two kids with zero adult interaction. I was their sole caretaker. They leaned on me for absolutely everything. Emotionally, physically, mentally. My son was struggling with the divorce and would cry at night, it was heartbreaking. I was 20 lbs. overweight and struggling mentally.

I hadn't been sleeping since the divorce was finalized, so I knew I had to do something. I decided to really dive headfirst into mindfulness and manifestation. I decided that the storyline I was telling myself was not serving me. I wrote myself a new mantra:

I'm worthy of love and I deserve a great, big, happy love. I'm worthy and deserving of a love centered on mutual respect, communication, and understanding. If I don't receive what I think I want, it's because something better is coming. I trust and have faith that god, the angels, and the universe are guiding me. I'm worthy and deserving of feeling abundant love. I am a creation of God and the highest — I deserve all of my desires. I attract big, happy love because I radiate it. Thank you, God, the angels, and the universe for always guiding me.

I decided that I would not chase or try to prove my worth, but I would take care of myself and allow love to be magnetized to me based on how I treated myself. I started working out again and meal-planning. I focused fully on self-care unapologetically. I was willing to put myself out there, but if I didn't receive what I thought I wanted, I knew something better would be coming for me. I embraced that belief fully. I wrote my mantra out in the notes section of my phone, and uploaded it as my phone background. Every time I picked up my phone, I would repeat my new mantra.

During this time, I leaned heavily on my sister for support. I was still struggling with sleepless nights. I made sure to ask "Do you have the mental space for me?" before I called her daily. She suggested that I join Tinder. I was hesitant at first, but she said, "You need something to occupy your time." So I joined. I made sure to add to my profile that I'm a single mother and I am not looking to mess around, so don't waste my time. I decided that I would ask the tough questions first, and I knew that anyone scared by those questions was not for me. I was determined not to force it. And I found myself swiping "no" on just about everyone. I think I swiped "no" on every person in Massachusetts until I was brought to one person from Rhode Island. I hesitated. I thought, "He looks like someone I wouldn't normally be attracted to." So I swiped right. Before I knew it, David was messaging me with the corniest joke I had ever heard. I asked the difficult questions right from the beginning: Do you smoke? Do you drink? Do you have kids? What would your ex say about your break-up? Do you want more kids? What's your favorite movie? What's your favorite food? He didn't smoke, didn't drink, and had one child. His ex would say they weren't right for each other but were good co-parents. He didn't want more kids, his favorite movie was *Once Upon A Time in New York*, and his favorite food was Italian. He wasn't scared away by my questions. He was responsive and happy to answer them. We talked all throughout the night over the next few days. On night three, however, we were talking about our favorite foods and the conversation ended a bit abruptly.

I didn't think anything of it and holding true to my "I will not force it," I went to bed figuring he would text me in the morning. When I woke up, he hadn't texted me. I went about my day, did my workout, spent some time outside with the kids, and thought, "He must have been talking to a few people and found one that he liked the best and it wasn't me." I remembered my mantra: if I don't receive what I think I want, it's because something better is coming. That night, I received an

Instagram message from someone I didn't know. The message read "I just want you to know, someone is using your pictures to catfish people on Tinder." At first, I thought "Wow! Someone thinks I'm pretty enough to use MY pictures?!" Then I noticed the last name on this Instagram account was the same as David's. I thought of our last conversation. I went back to read it. We were talking about our favorite food. I replied, "I'm a 95-year-old man and I have acid reflux, so I can't eat red sauce." And that is when he stopped responding. I realized that my statement could have easily been misconstrued. I wrote back "Is this my David? I am not a 95-year-old man, but I have acid reflux like a 95-year-old man." We laughed for a bit and I promised him that I was a real person.

We talked every night for a month before we met in person. On our first official in-person date, we got food and watched a movie. To my surprise, I fell asleep! I woke up scared that he would be upset with me, but he was asleep, too. I couldn't believe it. We had been talking every single day for two months, but this was the first time we had seen each other in person, and I FELL ASLEEP?! At first, I was beyond embarrassed. When I look back, I realize that my body knew before I did: that I was safe. We have been inseparable ever since. The more I learned about him, the more he checked off boxes on my list of "the perfect relationship." Did I actually manifest this man? I like to say that he was my first intentional manifestation.

I went through so much heartache in the 12 years I spent with my ex-husband. I was gaslit, told I was crazy, that I made things up, was made to feel insane. I hated who I became and I didn't like the totally different person I saw in the mirror. I am so happy that I mustered up the courage to leave that relationship. It was the most toxicity I had ever experienced. It's not all sunshine and rainbows now, but I can actually say I like who I am.

Since the divorce, I can set boundaries and stick to them, and use my voice. I have learned so much through mindfulness and manifestation practices, and I have met so many people who have affected my life positively. I chose myself. I chose to love myself and put myself first because I realized I could not pour from an empty cup. I learned that filling my cup first is not selfish, but necessary. I cannot give my best to others if I don't give my best to myself first. I like to say that I love myself wholly, completely, and fully. I know that the Universe has my back, favors me, and supports me. I have seen the evidence in my reality. Choosing myself was the best decision I have ever made. If I could give advice to anyone who is experiencing mental and emotional abuse, it would be to take the leap. Love yourself enough to get out of that situation. You are lovable, and you deserve to feel that deeply. When you don't believe, borrow my belief. There is someone out there who will treat you like you are the most perfect being ever created. In order to find it, you must be the first person to treat YOU like you are the most perfect being ever created. Practice this belief daily. Repeat the mantra daily. Love yourself wholly, completely, and fully in every single moment, even the ugly ones. We show others how to treat us based on how we treat ourselves. So put yourself on the pedestal, because you are the main character.

Jessica LaMontagne runs her own content strategy business as a social media strategist and mindfulness coach. With a Master's degree in Education, she brings expertise in education and social media, leveraging her experience to drive positive change. With a passion for personal growth and development, Jessica advocates for self-care and mindfulness. She believes in aligning passions with purpose and making a positive impact on the community.

ANN LYNCH

INNER HEALING FOR OUTER JOY

I remember as a little girl feeling like I was "different." I had an awareness that it was like I wasn't from here. I would see things from a different perspective, unlike the perspectives of the people I knew. Some might refer to this as an out-of-body experience. I just knew on a deep level that things for me and around me were different than what I was seeing and noticing with other kids. I was bullied, controlled, disrespected, and overpowered by others because of this.

Well, you might be asking or wondering what I'm referring to. The best way to describe this is when things become "too much" for me in any given environment, I would escape and go into the ether, as I will call it. This was due to the circumstances or situations occurring around me being just "too much." I would float myself above the space I was in and observe what was going on. I'd think, "This is crazy, these people are crazy, this is chaos."

There were times I couldn't even do that, meaning I wasn't adept enough for certain circumstances to even look down and comprehend what was happening. I would float up there and zone out, disconnecting myself from the reality I was in. It wasn't until much later in my life that I realized what I was doing in those moments, which you will hear about in the pages ahead.

I am the youngest of seven children. We would have been eight, but my mother had a miscarriage. That is all I know about that child. In that generation of the late '60s when I was born, things like miscarriage were not talked about openly. Now, I can imagine it was hard for my parents and ultimately my other siblings as well. But, back then when things were challenging or hard to deal with, or no one knew how to handle difficult situations, they were just ignored like it never happened, or swept under the rug sort of speak.

I learned from a young age through my environment that I didn't feel safe, heard, or valued. My father worked hard, and he was hard on us. My thoughts, feelings, opinions, needs, and wants weren't considered or honored. There is a saying I often heard as a young girl, "Children are to be seen, not heard." Well, that was ingrained in me. We grew up on a farm, and there were an overwhelming amount of chores we had to do, along with managing school, homework, and extracurricular activities. If it wasn't done in the way that he wanted it, it wasn't accepted and needed to be done again and better. If I questioned by saying, "Well, Dad I thought," and explained what I thought, I was told, "Well, don't think." We were not allowed to complain, cry, or show any emotion. That was so difficult for me being a sensitive child. It was extremely confusing to me as a little girl, and I felt like I was a prisoner within myself. This caused a limiting belief that "you are not smart enough and your thoughts are not valuable or worthy." Also, being the youngest played a role in those beliefs, too. I wasn't asked at times for my opinion or input, which left me feeling left out and dismissed. This carried into my adult life. I didn't know this back then. I was just learning how to survive in my environment.

Being the youngest of seven had its pros and cons, as any placement in a family does. Some of my siblings were a decade older than me, so I was exposed to chaotic situations that might have been expected at their age, but that made me feel unsafe as the youngest.

From my experience, I was taught to do what others wanted or requested of me. Like a true Pisces, I took on the energies and situations of my environment as well. It was like I had to be what others needed me to be at the time. So, I didn't know who I was.

I remember having to "escape," as I referred to earlier. I wasn't consciously "escaping" – it was what my body-mind was doing to protect myself. Science or mental health professionals would call this dissociation, according to *Psychology Today*.

Dissociating is the experience of detaching from reality. It encompasses the feeling of daydreaming or being intensely focused, as well as the distressing experience of being disconnected from reality. In this state, consciousness, identity, memory, and perception are no longer naturally integrated. Dissociation often occurs as a result of stress or trauma.

Depersonalization and dissociation are survival techniques used when a person is experiencing a traumatic event. Well, then we may ask, what is trauma? One definition of trauma is a disconnection from self. Gabor Mate is a Canadian physician and author specializing in addiction, stress, and childhood development. He explains that trauma comes from the Greek word "wound." In the movie *The Wisdom of Trauma*, Gabor speaks of "trauma as it is not what happens to you; it is what happens inside you as a result of what happens to you." I watched this movie when it came out in 2021. The movie reflects on the connection between illness, addiction, trauma, and society.

The movie was fascinating to view, as it allowed me to learn much more about myself, my family, my friends, and society as a whole, and understanding how childhood experiences mold and shape our lives. Trauma is the invisible force that shapes us. It shapes the way we live our lives, the way we love, and the way we make sense of the world. Trauma is the root of our deepest wounds. Our behaviors, diseases, judgments, and symptoms start in the wounded human body.

This movie helped to bring some pieces of the puzzle together for me. For me, being the youngest and having a brother 12 years older growing up in the '60s, I witnessed alcohol abuse in my family, and my brother, Mark, with drugs. My father would get very angry with my brother, and there were times when it got physical. My dog would get involved trying to protect one or both of them, and that would take it to a whole new level. The police would come to break it up, and they would take my brother away. I was very scared being that young girl at the age of five or six years old. Watching the fighting would create such tightness in my body; clenching in my jaw and stomach, fingers and toes. In this particular event, I didn't dissociate fully as I remember it. I stayed present and remember it quite vividly like it was yesterday. However, there were many occasions that I now understand were experienced in the physical, or Lodge In, and the dissociation and depersonalization would occur. Lodge In means the stress, trauma, and story were stored in my body to be uncovered later in life when I was in a safe enough place to uncover it and heal.

In the book *The Polyvagal Theory*, Stephen Porges speaks similarly to the work of Gabor Mate, *When the Body Says No*, which explores the role of the mind-body link in conditions and diseases, and the Bessler van der Kolk book, *The Body Keeps The Score*, in that the Body detecting states of safety or danger.

A simple explanation is that the body has three states of biological pathways.

1. Safe and Social Engagement – joyful, calm, settled
2. Flight & Fight – flee or defend
3. Shutdown & Immobility – fawn, freeze, and restrict

If one of these states is active, the others are dead or not accessible. For example, if one is in flight or fight mode, they are not able to be socially engaged.

All of these three states support our body's capacity for well-being and survival. The body-mind knows how to take care of itself in times of stress, trauma, grief, etc. The brain is ever-changing, and recovery from the body's storage of the stress and trauma that occurred previously that put one into the states of Fight, Flight, Freeze, or Fawn is possible. Fawning is a trauma response that uses people-pleasing behavior to appease an aggressor, avoid conflict, and ensure safety.

Biological states are unconscious, which means you don't choose your biological state. You don't choose to be in safe and social engagement, flight or fight, or shut down. These are responsive to the environment and the internal world. When we are young, our experiences shape and mold us. What is occurring at that time we are processing unconsciously from our circumstances.

Your body gets input from your five senses, and then your brain stem decides if it's safe, dangerous, or a life threat. Then shifts the body into one of the more defensive or safe states to survive or optimize its resources. All of these three states increase the body's well-being and chance of survival.

As we grow and mature, the body-mind is presenting itself to be healed and moved through. This shows as a layer of emotional defenses — anger, fear, sadness, guilt, and shame. When these present themselves, they appear as judgment, need to be right, blaming, not showing up, procrastination, freeze response, anxiety, grief/depression, neediness, overly sympathetic, I did or I "am" doing something wrong, confusion, conflict, regret, self-hatred, and more.

So, what happens is sometimes when it is too late, we realize there is more to uncover and heal, like an injury, an illness, chronic symptoms, body pain, or discomfort.

I learned all of this by going through it. I had pain and tightness in my body, and through yoga and meditation, I became more aware. Through somatic work, I am able to release the patterns of limiting beliefs to heal and live a better life. So, I have choice now, whereas before I wasn't "awake or I couldn't see it" because I was still in shutdown, freeze, or fawning and unable to notice what was really being uncovered.

What drove me to this was I was anxious, stressed, exhausted, unhappy, and had chronic symptoms and tightness in my body. I was searching for help. As I started to heal I uncovered this deeper learning and want everyone to know that "The Body Keeps the Score."

Throughout my life, I experienced many forms of abuse, including emotional, mental, physical, psychological, and sexual. In these experiences, my body-mind used the biological pathways to protect me through the dissociating, depersonalizing, immobilizing or fawning, and fighting when I was able.

I went to talk therapy at the age of 21. I wasn't happy and felt sadness and a heaviness in my body. I had exercised all my life, and as I was getting into my early 20s I realized that I only felt happy after I exercised. I knew that was because of the endorphins released, but in my mind, I "needed" to exercise daily to not feel anxiety, sadness, depression, and even stressful restlessness. The social worker suggested I keep exercising, as it was good for me to do so.

Through yoga and meditation, I became more aware. Through somatic work, I am able to release the patterns of limiting beliefs to heal and live a better healthier life. So, I have a choice now, where before I wasn't "awake or I couldn't see it" because I was still in shutdown, freeze, or fawning state and wasn't able to notice what was really being uncovered.

My life started to change for the better once I found various healing modalities such as yoga, meditation, somatic coaching, spiritual healing, and practices for deeply connecting to myself.

I remember when I was eight years old and my stomach hurt, my mom took me to the pediatrician. He did his physical test of poking and prodding a bit with my mom there. He said to my mom, "I can't find anything. It's all in her head." Well, I was there and thought, "Oh wow, I am making this up?" This started my belief that "I can't trust myself and what do I know anyway?" As I got into my early 20s, I had many physical challenges, like digestive problems such as IBS, which was no surprise since I had stomach issues as a little girl, TMJ (temporomandibular joint pain) from clenching my jaw, back pain, inflammation, and more. In my 40s, I was experiencing adrenal fatigue, chronic fatigue syndrome to the point that I would fall asleep driving, and more. I started to see a naturopath after seeking many years of help from the Western world of medicine. However, I was carrying around a bag of supplements, trying different diets, and still not feeling better.

Although I stayed in talk therapy for 24 years, I didn't move forward in a way that helped me be happy and feel more connected to myself. It has been alternative healing that has given me the most healing, progression, and support.

What I have learned through my life is that our healing is a process of peeling back layers of an onion. Our healing and progression in this life is not a quick fix or a one-and-done. It IS a rinse and repeat of all the things that allow us to heal on all levels of our being, by supporting us, so we can live the life we want to live.

The truth is that through my healing and finding a connection to myself with the dedication to live a better, healthier life, I am back in the playing field. Some call this the "Great Work" by continuing the journey of self-discovery and evolution and stepping through the fear to heal and progress while healing all parts of ourselves. I am in the game, and it feels good. It is okay to be sensitive or affected by an environment and also be able to remove yourself from it. I believed that I was different in a bad way, that being sensitive and disconnected from self and spirit was bad. It is also true that I am not really alone in what I experienced, as many people do use depersonalization and dissociation to survive their circumstances. I am enough, I am loved, I am safe, and most importantly, I am in charge of myself. I am continuing to learn how to honor myself even when others don't know how to.

Ann Lynch is a somatic empowerment coach, author, healing practitioner, myofascial release practitioner, yoga expert, and the owner of Shine Your Light Healing and Yoga. Additionally, Ann is a Soul's Purpose Facilitator and the creator of the Gateway to Health program for stress reduction. She helps her clients connect to their voice and birthright of empowerment, health, joy, and worthiness.

Through Life Activations, Crystal Healing, and Ensofic Ray and Jikden Reiki, she helps people step out of anxiety, tightness, and tension in the body as well as chaos, confusion, and spiraling thoughts in the mind. Ann guides her clients to make aligned decisions, heal, transform, and create the life they truly desire to live. Her clients have referred to her as the "Pattern Breaker."

PAULA REARDON-WEBSTER

ENOUGH

A simple word, just six letters. So many vowels! Not an easy mark for SCRABBLE, and most definitely not an easy word to embody. "Enough." And yet this cute little six-letter, single-syllable word has been a tyrant in my life, generally in stealth mode, eventually letting me look it in the eye as it reared its bothersome head.

I need to acknowledge right off the bat that, as a sixty-plus-year-old woman who has had the privilege of participating in 12-step recovery for decades and in therapy for a bit longer, I see very clearly that "Enough" is not my booby prize to carry alone in this world. It is the door prize for many of us. That and its best friend "Not Worthy." Perhaps it's a gang that includes "Unloveable," and its many variants, just like a virus. It's a trademark for those of us who grew up in alcoholic homes and dysfunctional homes. Heck, a lot of those born into Western civilization are branded with these monikers upon birth.

My relationship with Enough started as a young child. One of my first memories is of vomiting on myself in the crib when I was perhaps two or three years old. I was old enough to eat "grown-up" food, as I remember what I had eaten (or what re-appeared) was Dinty Moore beef stew. My parents were downstairs in the kitchen drinking, so I knew not to disturb them by crying. So I didn't. I went to sleep in my pile of puke. Nice.

Dad suffered from the disease of alcoholism, and Mom was the penultimate co-dependent. She was a typical 1950s housewife and never did anything to rock the boat. Raised in an alcoholic home herself, she grew up post-depression and came into her adulthood during World War II. My mother defended her right to drink. It was the norm, in her family and in the world.

I thought the "problem" in my home was that my parents were older parents, as Mom was 44 and Dad was 45 when I was born. My sisters were nine and ten years older than me. I was a lonely, little, lost child. That was not typical but alcoholism was the problem.

Thank God for my best friend Chippy across the street. He and his Mom, Kathleen, were my guardian angels, and helped me "lighten up." In many ways, I felt like an only child, and it might have appeared that as a result I "got more." I got more isolation, and more dysfunction. Yet, there were some ways in which that was true; I got to go away to summer camp, as my mom knew it would be hellacious for her to have bored, little, lost me moping around.

Going off to camp was terrifying for me. Then again, every-thing was terrifying for me. I was terribly shy, kind of cute, and somewhat likable. In hindsight, camp was the perfect place for me to notice the sense of not belonging, and to try to find the right workarounds to fit in. I did OK at sports and I was quite good at tennis. I found a friend who was so gregarious; she took me under her wing and became my camp bestie for a few years. Suzanne's dad was a successful doctor. They invited me to go to Nantucket with them, but first I went up to New Hampshire and stayed at their home for a few nights. They had central air and a poodle – wow! They were rich! No one in my everyday life in Medford lived in that sort of luxury. We took a puddle-jumper flight out of Boston to Nantucket. My first flight – impressive! I started to think that having things might make me ENOUGH.

In high school, I immersed myself in the group of friends I hung out with during eight years of Catholic School (a whole other training in not being enough). We started drinking, some of us more so than others. And the truly cutting-edge pack puffed on pot and pipes, adding other substances down the line. I was addicted. Addicted to the sense of escape from not being comfortable in my own skin, addicted to this newfound sense of belonging, addicted to another way to feel "cool." Although I got killer grades (did I mention I was pretty bright academically? Of course not), I was a class officer, Student Council member, and held a bunch of jobs and other activities, including playing guitar and singing. All the while, alcohol was the glue holding me together.

Off I went to UMass Amherst, a big party school with amazing academics, attractive mainly for the former. I graduated Summa Cum Laude and passed the CPA exam. Sexy, right? I really got a lot of holes punched in the "Enough" card with academic prowess and activities. It seemed to validate me to tread the path of success. So I jumped into the business world as a 21-year-old aspiring CPA with my business suit, matching shoes, and handbag. I had arrived. As Steve Martin, jumping up and down, yelled in the movie, *The Jerk*, "I am SOME-BODY!"

There is a certain amount of truth to the idea that as we earn our own keep, make our own way in the world, and live on our own in the world, our self-esteem rises. I am a believer that self-esteem comes from esteemable acts. But I also know that this adulting thing, this living gig, is an inside-out job. As my career grew, my friend circle tightened, and I had a long-term relationship. But I was unable to commit to him. Our friends were getting married and buying homes. I was stuck with my head in the party world. My bookcase began to reflect my inner struggle as friends and family were giving me self-help books such as *Why Am I Afraid to Show You Who I Am?*

The twenties are the time of transitioning from young adult to adult; from mixed up to grown-up, separating from family, and finding your identity. I was grown-up all right, trading cheap wine and Molson beer for Dewars Scotch on the rocks — splash and a twist, please. At twenty-eight the boyfriend who I thought was "the answer" (I had started to realize I needed an answer, even though I did not know the question), the guy who wanted me to move in, to marry, to grow up and grow old with, dumped me and told me I had "too many problems for any one person to be expected to handle." I was heartbroken; he drove a Mercedes.

After that, the most unlikely thing happened; the grace of God entered my life, and I landed in recovery from alcoholism within a week. Brought to my first meeting by a family member, I found a bunch of motley drunks who were the most spiritual people I could imagine. If you are familiar with Twelve Step programs, there is a collective penchant for trite sayings. "Expect a Miracle" is one of them, and day by day, I was a miracle. I did not feel like one, but I did not drink or take drugs, eventually, I quit smoking (no big deal, just two-plus packs a day), and I was drawn into the steps of recovery, where I learned how critical self-awareness is. Taking an honest look at myself with the support of others, learning to ask for help (from people and from a Higher Power), learning to live in the day, forming new connections, and really stepping into a whole new way of life, I started down the path of being the 2.0 version of Paula.

The trajectory of becoming was slow and steady for me, but putting one foot in front of the other, life gradually got better. But anxiety was always lurking in the background, I was not aware that the soundtrack to my life was stuck on "The Inner Critic" channel pretty much always. I should have been promoted sooner. I should have taken that other job, should have finished my MBA, should have gotten married already – when I had the chance. The big stuff was fodder for self-flagellation. And all the small stuff was as well. I swam against the tide with therapy, prayer, and meditation, and whatever self-help program came along. I was doing OK being me.

At 38, I took the plunge and got married; I was in love with my husband and he with me. There were a number of issues he hadn't dealt with in his own traumatic upbringing, but that's OK; I can help with that! He was and still is a good man. The only thing better than one person who feels like they are not enough is two people together! Working as the controller at a renowned hospital, my career was going well, and hubby's HVAC business started growing by leaps and bounds. We were quite a team. He might have been a wee bit more intense than me, but I was up for this busy, busy life. I actually fell in love with "busy," which feels like a healing balm for not enough.

We decided to start our busy family, but we were to hit some speed bumps. There were a couple of lost pregnancies and some subsequent unsuccessful infertility treatments. Wow! Talk about feeling like not enough. I had witnessed a co-worker adopt a baby from China, and our friendship grew through her process, which soon became our process. This was a pivotal point for me (and many) where the clarity of what's truly important starts to drown out the rest of the noise. Two beautiful, adorable babies, two years apart, two trips to China, two adoption groups, gifts from my Higher Power. And there was plenty of room — oodles of room, really — to feel not enough and to try to be and do more.

When my daughters were young, I left my career and became a full-time mom; it is a privilege to be able to make that choice. I set out to be an amazing mom and did not need to look far for examples of what to do, as we lived in a little suburban town with lots of "Type A" moms to watch. There were innumerable opportunities to provide service in the schools and the community and make frequent deposits to the "Bank of Enough." And my partner was working his own magic with enoughness, making lots of money, and looking at the outside stuff as what makes a happy home.

I can not say what day it was when I started saying "ENOUGH" to this enough ride. The anxiety was bringing me to my knees, literally. There was constant fighting in our home. I could not seem to do anything right. The kids were adolescents, not listening, and at times acting out. I lost any sense of who I was during those years. Having lost the identity of CPA and controller, I moved into the role of "Super Mom" and wife for a bit. Now that was gone. I felt disrespected invisible kind of worthless.

For a few years, I participated in a children's book writer's group and enjoyed learning this craft. It was fun, creative, and meaningful to me. A friend of mine was attending Graduate School at Lesley University. She suggested that I look at their creative writing program and take some classes. Why not? I was searching for my place, my purpose. When I looked at the graduate school website, a banner started flashing across the page — "Mindfulness Studies Graduate Degree or Certificate program starting!" Interesting. I was not a frequent meditator and knew consistency of practice would really benefit me. Then again, so would daily exercise and not eating quarts of ice cream. I felt compelled to check out the program on the website. For the next hour or so, I toggled between the Creative Writing Program and the description of the Mindfulness Studies program.

And then I looked down. I saw my fingertips tapping the keyboard. "Hey — what's going on down there?" I wondered. Turned out the fingertips were registering me for a class in the Mindfulness Studies Program in the Graduate School of Arts & Social Sciences. Just like that, I was on a new path. The first class was "Mindfulness Theory and Practice," combining daily mindfulness practice and journaling with learning the history of meditation in the West, and the neuroscience regarding why this works. I didn't need a neuroscientist or a functional MRI to tell me that, in thirty days, the daily committed practice had made a mark on my central nervous system. Despite the fact that nothing had changed in my home, with my husband and kids, that no outside circumstances had shifted, I felt so much calmer. I no longer felt like a walking anxiety attack.

On to the next class, week-long silent retreats, and applying to the master's degree program. On to teaching some community groups, running day-long retreats with colleagues, serving on the Board of Directors at a regional mindful schools program, and leaning into teaching for them. Taiji-Qigong instructor certification and teaching classes came next. Then a 500-hour yoga teacher training. And you guessed it, many more trainings and certifications. Have I found a new place of More to fill up Enough?

Yes and no. Mostly no, but definitely some yes.

Shortly after starting the graduate program, my husband and I separated, and eventually, we decided to divorce. I was devastated. In my head, I knew it was for the best, but my heart was broken, and our family as we knew it was forever changed. Friends would comment on how amazing I was to be attending graduate school while going through this trauma. Are you freakin' kidding me? Mindfulness practice and the study of it were the glue that was holding me together. I was so up close and personal with those voices — the inner critic, the saboteur, the desperado — that I couldn't see before, and therefore I believed them to be true. I learned not to believe everything I thought. Or perhaps not to believe any of what I thought. I was shaken and shaky, but I could see it and not have to run from those feelings. I did not magically become a new person, but I felt a gradual opening, a softening, a becoming.

At times it felt like I found a magic elixir, and I wanted to share it with as many people as I could. Mindfulness practice. Self-compassion practice. Qigong and Taiji, which are mindful movement practices to help shift and balance the body and energy. I was teaching and I liked it, possibly loved it, and I was pretty good at it. It lights me up to see other people light up. Those keyboard-clicking fingertips sent me on a path of new purpose and work in the world.

The training continues. It seems to be like potato chips. Bet you can't eat just one! I am able to check my motives in this area, for the most part. *The Course in Miracles* talks about "the ego speaks first and loudest." I run up against that ego all the time, but can often see you there, you trickster.

I happen to know by observation that those on a path of healing and coaching and teaching and sharing are prone to being life-long learners, which is a beautiful way to re-frame continuous training. I am learning to slow down a speck. I am learning to leave a little more space in my life, taking time for savoring and appreciation. I am learning to love more deeply, which I believe is why we are here. I am including myself in those I love. I am (for the most part) comfortable in my own skin, and I walk this world with greater openness and open-heartedness than I ever thought was possible, with the caveat that I am a work in progress. Others show me how to do this, with dignity and grace.

And I am starting some new work, taking a new direction, and combining a multitude of interests to create intergenerational programs. I see the need for this and feel inspired because I am paying attention to myself and to the world. Sometimes I start thinking that what I create needs to be more; that I need to reach more people, do some really big things, some really great things.

And then I remember that, if I can touch a few people's lives, share with them some tools for their journey, and witness the growth and path to authenticity in others here and there, that would be enough. *Truly ENOUGH.*

Paula Webster is a beacon of emotional intelligence and an authentic architect of community. Drawing on her personal experiences of overcoming loneliness and a sense of alienation, she fosters a sense of purpose, belonging, and kinship for others, through mindfulness and mind-body instruction, transformational coaching, and the creator of "Nowpoint" intergenerational programs and community through practice and storytelling. Paula empowers individuals to channel their inherent goodness and resilience, actively shaping a more compassionate world.

Christine

CHRISTINE SKUBON

THE PRICE OF PERFECT

I always thought I would get married and start having kids right after college. It's all I knew I really wanted. Everything else — a career, where I lived, what I did for fun as an adult, etc. was unclear when I thought about the future. But falling in love and spending the rest of my life with my "perfect" man? I thought about that constantly, and every boy I liked from seventh grade on was potential true love in my eyes.

I met him when I was 27 at a friend's Super Bowl Party. It was my first public appearance since my breakup with my live-in boyfriend. He was five years my junior, and I was terrified that I was "too old" to find that man I had dreamt of for so long. My self-esteem was awfully low and I was a mess.

This new potential prince was the brother of my friend's boyfriend, so I trusted him sooner than I would have trusted a complete stranger.

We hung out a few more times with that same group before

he asked his brother for my number. He had a successful career and owned a house, came from a big family, was raised in the same city as I was, and wasn't just looking for a fling. At that point in my life, he was exactly what I was looking for, even if he was 13 years older than me and had been married before.

So when he called and asked me out on a REAL date, like pick me up and take me to a nice restaurant for dinner, I was thrilled. My generation didn't do this "real date" thing at the beginning. We hung out here and there, usually in groups, and eventually relationships formed. Once you were officially in a relationship, then you went out as a couple. I was so entranced and felt so special that he chose ME to take out.

After that first date, things moved quickly. Before long, we were official and a few months later he asked me to move in with him. I was living alone and could barely afford my living expenses, and I was infatuated with this man, so I said yes. We hadn't said "I love you" yet, which gave me pause, but not for the reason you might think. I wasn't worried that it wouldn't last because I didn't love him or we hadn't known each other long enough. I was worried that he would change his mind, lose interest, and break up with me. In my head, if he told me he loved me, none of that would happen.

Over those first few months, he showered me with attention, took me places, and spent money on me. Money that neither I nor the guys I dated had to spend. He was confident, outgoing, and got along with everyone. There was one incident at my apartment early on that concerned me, but I convinced myself to ignore it as a one-off incident. We were on the couch watching TV and I said something sarcastic to him in a teasing way. My sense of humor is full of sarcasm and dry wit, so this was normal for me. He got angry and said he would leave if I kept talking to him like that. I immediately backpedaled and apologized profusely. I was so afraid of him leaving me, I would have done anything to keep him happy. This was the first time he was able to manipulate me into doing exactly what he wanted; begging him to stay and changing my behavior to appease him. This pattern would continue throughout our relationship and marriage, but on a much larger scale.

After I moved in with him, he eventually told me he loved me, but not until after I asked. Things were OK for a few months after we moved in together. We both had demanding jobs and were just getting to know each other while living together. But I started to see things that scared me a little bit. In hindsight, I should have put my back up a bit more than I did. For example, on a walk one day, I jokingly teased him again, probably with sarcasm. Instead of replying or speaking to me, he just took off running. I did not follow because I'm not a runner. Turns out he was very angry with me and reminded me that I was not to speak to him that way if I expected him to stay with me. My own insecurities constantly came into play, because my worst fear was being left by my significant other. So anytime he decided to dictate how my behavior should be in order to keep him, I immediately changed my behavior.

After living together for a while, we started to talk about marriage, and, as mentioned previously, I had just left a relationship before I met him. One of my fears at that time was that I was almost 30 and terrified that I wouldn't be married before then.

So when he asked me to move in with him and then asked me to marry him, I didn't give it a second thought. He was enabling my dreams to come true. I planned the wedding all on my own. He wanted nothing to do with it, saying he just wanted me to do it, because I was good at it and would do a better job than him, and he knew how much I liked it. Throughout our engagement, his behavior toward me became more and more demanding. But I kept making excuses for him because I believed that he loved me and that he was going to "save" me. I'm not exactly sure what I thought he was saving me from, perhaps a life alone? Which apparently was more terrifying to me than living with an abuser.

I had some best friends who were amazing, and they supported me as much as they could in all of my wedding planning and my relationship with this man. But at one point, my best friend sat me down and asked me if I was sure I wanted to marry him. This was only a few months before our wedding, and I can now admit that when she asked me that question, there was a part of me that wanted to scream, "No, I do not want to marry this man. I don't know what I've gotten myself into, but I don't know how to get out of it." But I was too proud to say that. All I could think of was how much money had been spent and how much planning had been done. even though she told me everyone would understand. I still couldn't imagine doing that. So, I went through with the wedding. A few things stuck out to me from the wedding. When I went for a trial run for my hair, he specifically told me that he would not "allow" me to wear my hair all the way up. His first wife had done that without asking him, and he hated it so much because it didn't look like her. Instead of fighting him on that, I did exactly as he asked. At the actual reception, I barely saw him. I was with my friends, and he was with his. We danced together for our initial song, and maybe one other. Looking back, I can say I didn't actually want to be around him. By then was criticizing everything I did or said, making him very hard to be around.

I don't know how to explain how my life was living with this man without giving specific examples of how he treated me. I have blocked out a lot of our day-to-day interactions due to the trauma, but the big events still linger in my memory. He refused to go anywhere with me that involved my family or friends. Yet, I was expected to go everywhere with him, no questions asked. Anytime I went out with friends or family, he would tell me he was fine with me going without him. Then within an hour of me leaving, he would text me, harassing me about coming home. I never gave in to his demands of going home when he texted like that, and for that I am proud. However, I did let it torture me, worrying about what was waiting for me when I got home. Every single time I got home, he would get mad at me for being out and berate me for as long as he felt necessary. He would also sit around and do nothing while I was out, texting me to say he was bored, but as soon as I arrived home, he would get up and say he had stuff to do, leaving the room immediately. When I called him out on this, he would twist it around and tell me that I couldn't expect him to just be waiting for me when I finally got home and that maybe I shouldn't go out and do stuff when I had a husband at home. It was maddening.

My best friend and I planned a 30th birthday party for me at our house, working for weeks to throw a huge party for my family and friends. I was so excited and happy to be celebrating my birthday with everyone I loved.

About halfway into the party, my best friend's husband Carl arrived. He walked into the party and said something along the lines of, "I'm here now, so the party can start." Everyone laughed and we moved on. A few minutes later, I heard a commotion near the food. I walked up to see my husband slapping a full plate of food out of Carl's hand onto the floor and screaming at him that if he wanted to fight, they could go right now. Mind you, he was 43 years old at the time. Apparently, he took offense to Carl's comment, said he insulted him and his house, and needed to threaten him to show that he was mad. That was the end of the party. Almost everyone left immediately, and I was left with him, his mother, and a few of his friends. I was extremely upset and hysterically crying for a while, though I didn't accuse him of anything. By this time, he had me trained to never question anything he did or said. I knew if I did, I would pay the price. After the last few guests left, he immediately tore into me. He screamed and yelled at me for hours, accusing me of inviting Carl on purpose to mess with him, telling me that it was my fault all of that happened because it was MY friend's husband. This continued ALL NIGHT LONG. He woke me up out of a sound sleep multiple times during the night to yell and berate me some more. I can't remember when it ended, but I know by the end, he had forbidden me to see my friend ever again. I was so brainwashed that I didn't know how to defy him, so I called my friend, told her what happened and said we couldn't see each other as much anymore. I cannot imagine what she must have thought and how that must have hurt her. We were like sisters and did everything together until that day. After a few months, I started seeing her again, but it was always rushed and sneaky. Even after he knew I was seeing her again, it was always an issue. This is the biggest regret I have from this relationship. I let this man take away my person, my best friend, my confidant. Thankfully, she's an amazing human and we're still friends. But our relationship has never been the same.

So far, my entire story has taken place over a three-year period. Even after all of this, I stayed with him for another four years. If you have never been in an abusive relationship, it's hard to imagine how someone would stay in a relationship like this. I had none of the signs in my life that indicated I might be susceptible to an abuser. I came from a good family, my parents were and still are together, I had a degree in Psychology no less, and had a stable career by the time we met. Yet, it still happened. Narcissists are extremely manipulative and can be in complete control of you before you even realize what is happening.

While I was living through all of this, I had no idea he was a narcissist. I discussed everything that was happening ad nauseam with my parents and friends, trying to figure out why he behaved that way. I tried everything I could think of to change ME so he would like me better. I did everything he asked and everything in my power to not make mistakes, because he did not tolerate them. I lost weight when he told me I was fat, and countless other things that I cannot even remember. None of it mattered. Nothing I did was ever good enough for him.

As our relationship continued, things got worse. One time I was on my computer on Facebook chatting with a guy I worked with about something. I was also working on something else at the same time and was toggling between screens. He walked by and decided I was toggling so that he couldn't see what I was typing. He accused me of cheating on him, threw my chair to the ground, and screamed in my face. Another time, I got home from having dinner with my dad, and he looked at me, told me I was fat, and wouldn't have sex with me again until I lost weight. This started many years of disordered eating for me.

One night on my way home from work in a snowstorm, I got nauseous from the falling snow swirling and had to pull over and get sick on the side of the highway. When I got home and told him, he screamed at me because we were supposed to go to his parent's house for dinner and I was ruining it. Not once did he ask how I was or even believe I was actually sick.

All the stories I have shared so far are the big ones, the events that still stick out in my brain almost ten years after leaving him. There were so many other incidents that blended together in my memories of him, none of which are good.

It took me years to finally leave him. I knew two years prior to leaving that I wanted out but had no idea how to do it. I was terrified. I didn't know what he would do, but I knew it wouldn't be good, and when you're being controlled in every possible way by an abuser, it's hard to see your way out.

The beginning of the end started when he finally decided he was ready to start a family. I had wanted to start right away due to some fertility issues my mother had when she was a young woman. I was worried I would have the same issues. After about eight months of trying, I told him I wanted to contact a fertility clinic to get some testing done. They agreed to see me even though it hadn't been a year of trying, due to my family history. He agreed to let me go, but very adamantly told me that he would NOT be tested for anything because he was fine. Sure enough, the testing showed that I was in early menopause at the ripe old age of 33, and would need help conceiving. This was everything I had always been afraid of coming true, and he still refused to get any testing or come with me to any appointments. After a few months of shooting myself up with hormones daily and going to the doctor multiple times a week, I got pregnant. Even though I knew I didn't want to be with this man, my wish for a child overshadowed that. I was thrilled.

My joy didn't last long. I had an appointment at the fertility clinic at about nine weeks, and he was finally going to come with me to hear the heartbeat. I had asked my mom to come along as well and for that, I am forever grateful. There was no heartbeat that day. My baby had died. I was told that since it was Friday afternoon, I had to wait until Monday to call my regular OBGYN to schedule a D&C. So, I had to go home with my dead baby inside me. This was the single worst thing that has ever happened to me. My mother came home with me and I cried in her arms for hours. I got in trouble with him for this, but I didn't care. The D&C happened the following week, and I spent two weeks on the couch with no desire to do anything. I've struggled with depression my entire life, but I had never felt anything like this before. It was like the world had lost its color. Nothing mattered.

After the fertility clinic sent me home with my dead baby still inside me, leaving me on my own to figure it out, I made the decision to no longer use that clinic. There was one other fertility clinic in the area where I grew up, so I made an appointment with them. I can't remember if he came with me to an appointment or not, but after my initial appointment, he finally agreed to get tested for his fertility levels. The night before the appointment, he started a HUGE fight with me. He said the only way he would get tested was if I used my hand to get him to completion. I flat-out refused, so he yelled and screamed at me. I decided to cancel his appointment.

The following morning when I woke up, it was like a switch had been flipped. I no longer felt any love for this man, no longer felt afraid he would leave me, and no longer wanted him to so much as touch me. This was a completely new feeling for me. Even through all his abuse, I still wanted him to love and accept me. I had been telling myself for years that if I just did everything right, he would come around and just love me.

Knowing that I wanted to leave and no longer being afraid to do so changed a lot within our relationship. He sensed it somehow and started "acting" differently towards me. I say acting in quotes because it was just that, an act. He wasn't trying to change himself or learn anything about himself or our relationship. He was pretending to be nice so I wouldn't leave, even though I had said nothing about leaving. I'm not sure how he knew, but I believe narcissists have a sense of their victims, knowing when they're starting to lose control of them. I do not think my ex knew this consciously, but he somehow sensed it.

My miscarriage happened in mid-October 2014. The fight that happened surrounding his fertility testing happened in early December. That holiday season, my ex acted like a completely different person. He was doing everything in his power to make me feel loved; he came to a few family gatherings, agreed to have our parents over for a holiday meal that we cooked, and started spending more money than usual on me. He normally used money to control me. He was nicer than he had been in years. But I was still done. Nothing he did changed anything in my head or my heart. I was just waiting around until I could figure out how to get out of my marriage.

Even though I knew I was finally ready to leave after knowing for two years that I should leave, I was absolutely terrified of taking the steps to make that happen. The fear I had wasn't surrounding where I would go or what I would do on my own. The fear was solely based on not knowing what he would do when I left. More specifically, what he would do to me. While he had never been physically abusive up until this point, I knew not to put anything past him.

I didn't tell anyone I was planning to leave right away, because I was afraid I would lose my nerve. I was also afraid he would find out somehow. He had me running scared and constantly watching my back. I was living in a constant state of fear; my nerves were shot. After the New Year, I told my parents that I was planning to leave and brought some clothes and things I would need to their house. Thankfully, they have always been very supportive of me and told me that when I was ready, they would be there for me.

The thing that always surprises me when I look back is how I ended up leaving. Had you asked me prior, I would have told you I was going to plan the date ahead of time and have my support people ready and waiting for me. Instead, I decided on a random weekday in February, while I was at work, that I was never going back. He had started a fight with me because he had planned something for us that night without telling me, and I had dinner plans with a friend of mine. To him this meant I was cheating on him, and he started harassing me via text. Again, something just clicked and I sent a text saying something like, "I am not cheating on you, but if you want to talk about separating, we can do that." I immediately texted my dad and told him what I had done. I started crying hysterically from nerves and the release of finally having told him.

I never stayed at my house I shared with him again after that day. The day after I went back with my mom and uncle to get as much of my stuff as I could fit into their vehicles. I was terrified to go back there, afraid he would be there and somehow force me to stay. At the time I didn't realize how hard it would be to separate myself from him after years of his abuse.

The first few weeks after I left are a blur. I don't remember many specifics about that time due to all the trauma I had gone through and was still experiencing. I do remember he followed me around without telling me and would text me saying he had seen me out, accusing me of a plethora of things that I wasn't doing. I was scared to go anywhere alone and avoided it for a while. My entire family and circle knew what was going on and were on high alert because no one knew what he might try. While he never tried to come after me physically, the emotional abuse I had endured while living with him continued via text.

For a while, after I left him I was still seeing him. I couldn't completely cut myself off from him; codependency and abuse are common with victims when trying to leave their abusers. If it weren't for the strong support of my family and friends, I don't know that I would have been successful in the long run. He turned on the charm trying to get me back, making all kinds of ridiculous promises about how he would change and things would be better. He took me out to eat, took me shopping, and spent thousands of dollars on me. I'm pretty sure he thought he could buy me back if he spent enough. He thought spending time and money would make me want to go back to him, but it was the exact opposite. Every time we saw each other during that time, I felt myself withdrawing from him. I was finally able to say I didn't want to see him anymore. This did not go over well. He started sending me 60-80 text messages a day, and I was unable to ignore them. My ability to remove him from my life happened in very small steps.

During this time, he accused me of cheating on him repeatedly. He even told his family that's why I left. He convinced them all that I was the villain; the cheating wife. Narcissists are very charming, especially in the public eye, and they are very successful at convincing people that their lies are the truth. One of his favorite things to tell me during this initial phase of separation was that I wasn't allowed to start over and divorce him. I cannot remember his exact phrasing, but he said he wasn't giving me permission to leave, so I couldn't do it. In his mind, I belonged to him like property, and if he didn't say I could go, then I had no right to go. This gives you another peek into the mind of a narcissist. He truly believed he owned me and had full control over my life.

The scariest thing that happened during the six months after I left him was the day he showed up at my job. I was the branch manager of a local credit union. He walked into my office and shut the door. He then proceeded to quietly berate me and antagonize me until I was shaking and in tears. One of my coworkers called the police, thank god, and they came and escorted him off the property. I decided to get a restraining order against him. I was much stronger than I had been immediately after leaving him and was mentally ready to finally block him from texting or calling me. I always had the ability but had been too scared of his retaliation. In order to get the restraining order, I had to print out every single text message and email he had sent me since I left. There were over 60,000 text messages and thousands of emails. I was granted a temporary restraining order, making it illegal for him to contact me in any way.

Once the restraining order was in place, I was able to focus on rebuilding my life. I was finally in a place where he wasn't controlling me, which felt so freeing. There was a time when I never thought I would be able to get away from him, and here I was doing just that. And I was thriving. I was working out regularly, spending more time with family and friends than I had in years, and I had my own apartment! While I was still dealing with the legal parts of divorce, I had completely removed this man from my life six months after leaving him. This is the greatest accomplishment of my life. It was the hardest thing I ever had to do, and I am so proud of myself for being able to leave.

Many women (and men) do not have the happy ending I had and are never able to leave their abusers. This is not their fault. The psychological ramifications of living with a narcissist (or any type of abuser) are intense and long-lasting. When you're living it, it seems like the only way you can survive is to just do as they say and try to be "good." I now know that if I was a different person, I probably would never have left. Narcissistic men prey on women with low self-esteem, who don't have a lot of support in their lives, and who may not be as intelligent as they are. In my case, he made a mistake. I did have low self-esteem about my body and physical appearance, but I did NOT have low self-worth. I knew life was worth living, and I had very specific ideas about how I wanted to live it. I had very strong ties to my family and a large circle of friends. These people never abandoned me and were continuously there for me, even when I wasn't there for them. I am forever grateful to all of them. I also have a very strong personality. No matter how often he tried to push me down, I pushed back and argued. He was never able to fully break me. I know this was his goal, as is the goal of all predators with their victims.

I am happy to tell you that I have been free of this man for nine years and I have never looked back. I am happily married with a seven-year-old daughter, who is the light of my life. I thank the universe every single day for giving me my husband and daughter, because I know I'm one of the lucky ones who escaped and found happiness again. I have also done a lot of healing over the years in many different forms. Leaving an abuser is the hardest part, but there is still so much work to do in the aftermath. I am in therapy and have been on and off since I left him. I have done a lot of reading on narcissists and people who left and survived. There is so much to be learned from the stories of others who have lived in your shoes. In the last two years, I have taken up yoga and strength training, which have helped me more than I ever thought possible. Quieting your mind and moving your body will do wonders to help heal the parts of you that you didn't even know needed healing.

I'll leave you with this. There is always someone out there who wants to help you. Even when you think you're alone in this world, you are not. During my marriage to this man and in the six months that followed, I relied heavily on the people in my circle, but I also found help from strangers in places I never expected. I know that's because I wasn't alone in this experience. Too many of us have experienced situations like this (or know someone who has) and are willing to help immediately without asking any questions or knowing a thing about you. There is still so much kindness and love in this world, and it is there for you when you need it.

Christine Skubon is a certified Integrative Nutrition Health Coach, who studied a holistic health and wellness program with the Institute for Integrative Nutrition. Her passion has always been helping people. The combination of her love of nutrition and overall wellness has provided Christine an opportunity to work with women to empower them to reach their wellness goals. She believes women coming together and sharing their experiences can change lives and the world. She is so honored to be a part of this amazing collection of Soul Stories.

JOANNE QUEENEY

LESSON FROM MY SON: LOOK UP & LISTEN

When I was asked to write my story, I immediately responded, "I don't have a story." I live a wonderful life full of family and friends. I have a successful career, appreciate life, meditate, and have learned to enjoy the pleasure of the present moment. However, I was quickly reminded that everyone has a story. It made me think about my life. Although I have experienced tragic loss at a young age, have had to deal with family and friends with alcohol and drug addictions, and have worked through a divorce, and a high-powered, time-consuming job, I am so grateful and happy. How did I get so lucky? Was it luck, or is there an underlying journey that I am hesitant to reveal? Well, that's the purpose of this chapter, to uncover and share the challenges that have led to growth and healing.

One key thing that you need to know about me is that I am a head-down, get-it-done kind of person. I stay focused and am constantly analyzing how to make things better. Both at work and in my personal life, I make sure everyone around me is taken care of and generally say "yes" to everything that is asked of me. People count on me. This expectation and behavior started at a very young age. And as I dug deeper into my past, I can see how this has shaped my life.

I am the youngest of four sisters and grew up in a middle-class family. I experienced loss at a very young age. My oldest sister passed away when I was two in a tragic car accident at 16 years old. She was a straight-A student ready to go to medical school. Aunts and uncles had to take care of me and my other two sisters for months, as my parents were in shock for quite some time. My second oldest sister also passed away at the young age of 33, when I was 23. As my family and I started to learn to live life without her, another tragic incident happened. My second oldest sister was electrocuted while blow-drying her hair and passed away. The same hair dryer and electrical outlet I used only moments before. This time I was old enough to truly experience my parents' grief. The words "Why didn't God take me" were spoken by my mom on a daily basis.

My parents' grief of losing two daughters put them into protection mode. I was not allowed to play over friends' houses or go to sleepovers. Everyone had to come to my house. My curfew was the earliest out of all of my friends. I was not allowed to go anywhere in a car without my parents. My mom would walk our dog to check up on me when I was out playing. My friends thought this was creepy, and I was embarrassed. However, we didn't understand what grief and the pain of losing not one child but two can do to a parent. I grew up knowing my parents' eyes were on my back at all times. But what I didn't know was how to feel. Death was not talked about in our home and neither was how to cope. Everything was swept under the rug to avoid painful discussions. I just kept my head down and did what I was told. I followed the rules so I didn't cause my parents any further pain.

The death of my second sister pushed me into the role of caregiver, not only for my parents but for my 18-month-old nephew. My sister chose to be a single mom and did not even tell the father of her son. Although I was just accepted to law school, I had to make the decision to forgo my dream at the time to be a lawyer. Life was not about me anymore. I fully committed to being a parent at 23 years old. I took on the challenge and put my whole heart and soul into the needs of my family.

It wasn't long after that my third oldest sister had a daughter. She was also a single parent but with added struggles of her own. She was a drug addict. My third oldest sister was unable to take care of herself or her daughter. She neglected the basic needs of her child and allowed a friend to get involved in her care. I, fortunately, realized that the friend was trying to get custody of my niece. Thankfully, I was in the right place at the right time to avert custody being handed over to the friend. I stepped in and became the guardian of my niece. I couldn't understand how any parent would not put their child first. It wasn't until later that I learned more about PTSD and drug addiction and the role this played in my sisters' ability to think clearly and make rationale decisions. Regardless, I remained head-down and focused. I had a role to play and a job to do.

During this time, I also learned a lot about alcoholism, not from my family but from my best friend. I committed to supporting her as well, and we navigated this disease together. I am her son's godmother, and he has lived with me intermittently for many years. He is a part of my family and joins us on all of our vacations. Watching the impact of alcoholism alter a parent's ability to care for oneself and their child is heart-wrenching.

So, in a nutshell, I was taking care of my parents, raising my nephew, niece, and godson while helping my sister and best friend through their addictions. There was no time to think about my needs or well-being. My life was taking care of others. I never had the time to listen to my inner voice that cried out for help, to slow down, and to take care of myself.

While I was trying to bring some normalcy to my family life, I continued to have the desire to learn and the drive toward a successful career. Having an education was not pushed on me by my parents. Neither my mom nor my dad graduated high school. My dad was drafted in the war, and my mom had to stay home to take care of her brothers and sisters. She grew up in a large Italian family with 12 kids and was a caregiver for her parents and siblings. I guess that's where you can say I got it from. She took care of them. I took care of her.

As a teenager, I worked at a healthcare insurance company and learned quickly that if I kept my head down and worked hard, I would get recognized. I moved up the corporate ladder quickly, however, the higher I got, the more challenging it was to compete in a white collared business full of men. But I was determined to succeed. In my first year as a managing partner for a global research and advisory firm, I received an award. When I walked to the podium and realized there were only a handful of women in the room, I was filled with pride. Traveling on a plane every week and working nights and weekends was paying off. However, I found that it was a big price to pay. The price was at the expense of not being "present" with my kids.

During my career, I got married and had two children – a son, Jake and a daughter, Jessie. To compensate for my long hours of working, I made sure to volunteer at their schools and extracurricular activities. I was the PTO president, coordinated events, and had an open-door policy with all of their friends. Our house was the go-to house to play at. There was a trampoline, in-ground pool, hot tub, cabana with a TV, and refrigerator full of water and soft drinks. Oh, and the full basketball court which converts to a pickleball court, too. My kids and their friends knew they were always welcome to come and have fun, enjoy a meal or two, and choose from a large freezer full of ice cream in the garage. No need for an ice cream truck when you were at the Queeney house. Like my parents, I wanted my house to be the place where kids can come and be a kid.

My house wasn't perfect all the time. When the kids were seven and five, I got a divorce from my husband, who remained my friend and an active parent in our kids' lives. We never talked about the divorce in our house. We just went on with our lives and ensured it did not impact the kids' daily lives. I realize now that I was doing the same things as my parents. Sweeping things under the rug.

DEFINING MOMENT

I had everything under control, so I thought. I was on my couch typing away on my laptop trying to finish a work project. My son was talking to me and I think I was just "yessing" him. Then I heard his sad voice, "Mom, you're not even looking at me or listening to anything I have to say."

In that moment, I felt a tear in my heart. He was right. I was focused on my work, and I neglected to look up and listen. That was the defining moment when I decided I needed to get my head out of the daily grind, allow myself to feel, and stop being a robot in my daily life. At the time, I thought coordinating themed birthday parties was a way to connect with my kids. Yes, I was the parent who did not just have cake and ice cream. There were ponies, jumpy houses, and mechanical bulls. I also made sure we went on vacations as a family. Making memories was important to me. However, all the great parties and vacations could not provide my kids with what they needed — for me to be present every day, look them in the eye when we talked, and genuinely listen to what they had to say. It sounds easy, but I needed help. My whole life was helping others, and now I needed to ask for help to learn to take care of myself. But where do I turn for help with an invisible struggle? Externally, everyone thought my life was perfect. But internally, there was something that was not right. I was failing to look deeply within, express my feelings, embrace grief, and look more at my inner wisdom than the screen. I needed to disconnect from my current way of life to reconnect with the family and friends that I love. I had to reset my mental and physical health and gaze at the vastness around me and nature's magnitude.

DISCONNECT TO RECONNECT

I knew that making a change meant that I had to focus on resetting my lifelong habits and shifting my mindset. The only way to do this was to step away from the daily grind and retreat to a place that supports my physical, psychological, and spiritual well-being. Health and wellness was in its infancy of being understood, and the mention of meditation made people's eyes roll. I recalled reading about a health and wellness spa called Canyon Ranch many years ago. It intrigued me, but it was expensive. I was constantly writing checks for my kids' activities, like football, basketball, cheerleading, and volleyball. However, I was struggling with justifying making an investment for my own well-being.

In December 2018, I decided to invest in a gift for myself, a four-day stay at Canyon Ranch. I wanted to go alone as to get a full experience without outside influence. This gift started my journey to lifting my head up, bringing back my body to the sensory pleasures of the present moment, and listening to my inner voice. It allowed me to just breathe and quiet my mind. I signed up for a "soul journey," where I had to stop putting on a brave face, tackle my demons, and open my mind to achieve pure joy. I am not a crier, but I let it all out during a sixty-minute session that day.

I loved every minute and was hooked on health and wellness. I became a member of Canyon Ranch and travel to their Arizona and Massachusetts locations many times throughout the year. I try and bring as many friends as I can to expose them to spirit walks, connect them with the idea of taking care of one's mind, body, and soul, and try something different that they have never done before. It surprised me that the concept of prioritizing self-care to reenergize your zest for life is not known by many. I wanted to share my experience with everyone that I talked to. I had a vision and designed a wellness center on a small piece of paper. The challenge was how to bring a place for renewal, wellness, and happiness closer to home and make it affordable for people to invest in themselves.

I googled "meditation near me" and found the WeBreathe Wellness Center, an inclusive Zen Retreat Center just two towns over.

I scheduled a private Chakra Clearing and Crystal Balancing session with the owner, Jenn. She was such an inspiration. She has created a studio that offers healing and coaching services and established a collaborative for women to make meaningful connections with one another and lift each other up in an authentic way. I joined her tribe of like-minded people to continue to find balance, be inspired, and feel supported. I am also involved in the formation of a new non-profit, WeBreathe Wellbeing Soul Sanctuary, to create a space for serenity and transformation. My passion and energy will be on bringing my drawing of a wellness center to life with a group of amazing people.

TRUE TRANSFORMATION

My story of wellness transformation will continue. I still take care of family and friends, but in a better state of mind. I make eye contact, listen more, talk less, say "yes" to things that make me feel good, and never feel selfish in taking care of myself first. I do not want to push my beliefs on anyone, but I truly believe finding yourself first will help you to help others.

For my son Jake, who allowed me to start my healing journey, I am so proud of the responsible and generous man he has become. I get great pleasure watching him embrace health and wellness as a twenty-year-old. He often reminds me of the words I instilled in him at an early age: "stay positive, and you can achieve anything you set your mind to."

For my eighteen-year-old daughter Jessie, who has a joyful nature and brings a smile to everyone she connects with, she teaches me to continue my transformation through her positive attitude. I asked her for a quote about something she has learned from me. Keep in mind she hadn't even read anything about my story. It brought a tear to my eye: "I do not think you realize how you have always had this mindset, but the meditation and everything you do has helped to bring it out. Jake and I are so inspired by you."

For anyone reading my story, I would like you to understand that sometimes it doesn't take one big challenge like addiction, divorce, or a tragic loss to make the decision to invest in yourself; it may just take a few simple words from a child - look up and listen.

Joanne Queeney is a Managing VP at Gartner, a global research and advisory firm. Joanne has over 40 years of healthcare experience providing direct, on-demand IT and business analysis, and advice to healthcare and government agencies. Joanne aims to take her experience in health & wellness and behavioral health from a corporate/technology perspective and shift it to real-life application after the realization that leveraging technology does not support the mind, body, and soul for joyful and healthy living.

The main concept behind the mind-body-spirit connection is that we are more than just our thoughts. We are also our bodies, emotions, and spirituality. Combined they give us identity, determine our healthcare, and make us who we are. Being part of the board for WeBreathe Well-Being Soul Sanctuary will allow for a broader focus and support for all as we journey toward a healthy mind, body, and spirit.

JACQUELINE DAVIS

LEARNING TO NAVIGATE ON MY OWN

I was born to a single teen mom in the partying stage of her life who wasn't ready for me mentally or physically. As the second youngest of 14 children, she was treated like a baby by everyone and was immature when she had me. My father wasn't allowed to be in my life, nor did he want to be. He was young, like my mother, and didn't have the capacity to take care of himself. He grew up in an abusive environment, and his father was a convicted pedophile. My mother didn't want him around, and my grandmother forbade it.

There was talk of my uncle taking me, because he and his wife wanted another baby. Although my grandmother adored me, she was exhausted from raising her own 14 kids. My grand-father, however, couldn't give me up. So I ended up as my grandparents' 15th child.

My grandma was an incredible and hard-working woman. She dropped out of high school to raise her eight siblings after her own mother passed away. When she was done raising her own kids, she joined the workforce as a military nurse.

I was the favorite, the "angel." But I was a very sick baby and was hospitalized constantly at Children's Hospital on and off until I was eight years old. Fevers, belly aches, and ear infections that had me screaming all the time. I was a horribly uncomfortable baby. After six months of all types of tests and evaluations, I tested positive for leukemia. My family was devastated. A few days later, they tested me again, resulting in a negative test. The first test result had been false positive. I had pneumonia four times.

I was an extremely sensitive kid and cried all the time at everything. My grandfather was my best friend. I idolized him. He walked me to the school bus stop each day and would pick me up early once in a while because he missed me and wanted to do something special with just me. When I was around five or six, I started having intuitive feelings about things and people, and I started saying things out loud that people found disturbing. I once told my grandmother's boss very matter-of-factly that he was going to die soon. My grandfather explained to me that those types of statements were really scary and hurtful to other people. So I stopped, and was too afraid to open up again for a while. Every so often, my intuitive gifts would appear, and I remembered my grandfather's warning and I'd shove them back down. Sometimes I thought I was going crazy. I never had anyone to discuss them with, so I kept it to myself.

I was close to my grandma too, but to me, she was a very scary and hard woman who never showed emotion. Her motto was "toughen up and never let people see your weaknesses."

She was very strict. I was never allowed to be alone with anyone she didn't know. I think this made me scared of people for most of my life.

Although biologically I was an only child, I was raised with cousins who teased me without mercy. I was the favorite, and I was quiet, and they were jealous. They thought I was crazy because I was saying all these crazy things, like "Aliens are coming to Earth."

School was also hard. I was quiet, so people spoke for me, which left me with nothing to say. I was keenly observant of people and often overwhelmed by them. Kids bullied me constantly. They called me names, threatened me, beat me up, and pushed me down the stairs.

The things I said scared them. I would call people out on lies, because I knew the truth. I knew when people were sick and could sense outcomes. When I was right, kids would freak out.

I really had no friends during middle and high school. I left public school to go to a private Catholic school. Ironically, the school was built on a cemetery, so although I had no idea what was going on, I was receiving all kinds of messages and information. This kept me from making friends, and I still got bullied. The loneliness and lack of acceptance drove me to completely give up on life. I really didn't want to be here anymore. Why live to be tortured, I thought.

My mom and my Uncle Charlie, who was an Elvis Presley impersonator, also lived at my grandparents' house with me. My mother often told me she couldn't stand the way I was. "I hate you. I really just don't like you," she'd say. She told me I was in the way, and if she wasn't my mother, she would never be friends with me. Like my cousins, she was jealous. I had the life and attention she wanted from her parents. Sometimes she left for days at a time to get away from me.

I struggled a lot and kept to myself and my dogs. They understood me and were a welcome distraction. I received nothing but unconditional love from them.

I was 12 when my grandma passed away. I remember being in the room with her at the end, and she was looking into space a lot. She couldn't speak much anymore, but she told me I was her sensitive baby and asked my family to be extra careful with me.

I ended up over the course of years meeting a few people I trusted enough to tell, and they were amazed. I thought no one was listening to me. But it happened, and they keep coming back. I had a friend take me to Salem for a party at a store called Omen. I told him about my intuitive feelings and how things were haunted, and they explained how I attracted spirit and I was coming into my gifts. I really never believed it.

I dated a few men here and there, but nothing was ever serious until my 30s when I met a man who was a friend of a friend. I hesitated to go but felt obligated to my friend. I remember being scared of him at first and ignoring my intuition. The first year or two were nice. When things were good, they were great. Then he started twisting everything I said, manipulating me, starting fights all the time. The relationship lasted another three years. I had no idea what was happening. I was being emotionally and mentally abused and had almost no idea until the end. It ended with him leaving me on the side of the road, raped and topless. We did have one date at the beginning where we went for a walk in the Arboretum, a place I always went for security and peace, and something yelled at me. It wasn't human. Not only yelled, but tried to chase me out of the park. I wish I had listened. At the end of the relationship, I was very sick with constant fevers and feeling moody. I couldn't eat. I looked horrible and was angry for no reason. I was also on the search for something to fix it but felt defeated and dead. I really think I spiritually died during this time. I felt completely numb and didn't give a shit about anything. I cried daily and at moments asked God to take me.

One day while browsing Facebook, I saw an ad for a meditation session and I asked what it was. The woman who posted about it inboxed me to invite me. At first, I thought she was fake, but then thought oh well, I really have nothing to lose. I got to her office, and I was petrified and hugely skeptical. There were three people there, and everyone was warm and welcoming. I could tell that they sensed the pain I was in. They gave me Reiki, and although I didn't feel much, my moods started to shift. They asked me to give Reiki in return. At first, I was hesitant, but they said I was a natural, so I decided to try.

The following day, Holly, the practitioner, invited me to her office to talk. She started to explain things to me about energy and being an empath and how she was a shaman and believed that I was, too. She said I was a natural and took me under her wing of love and protection. I ended up in her office a few times a week. It became my home, and the beginning of my spiritual journey. I finally had my first place where I could tell people about the visions I had and what I felt. I stopped thinking I was crazy. Holly attuned me, and I fell even more in love with energy and healing. I grew hungrier for healing and furthering my spiritual journey by exploring what I was capable of. I got my Level II Reiki training, and it changed me. I was scared to practice, still afraid of being seen and being laughed at. I decided I needed to jump in. An ad came up during Mercury Retrograde for Reiki at Open Door Studios in Braintree. I decided to take action without overthinking.

On my first day, I was petrified. I walked through the door with my heart beating and my confidence very low, wondering if I belonged there. I saw a gentleman at the counter with long hair. I knew him, but I wasn't sure how, and I was very intimidated for some reason. Maybe I knew he would help me continue to remove my mask to reveal my authentic self. I ended up talking to him and realized he was going to be my first client. I was scared, but when I finished he said he was very impressed and encouraged me to explore my gifts, that I was well advanced. More advanced than I believed, and I should continue to explore my abilities. Over the next couple of weeks, John talked often about the Spiritualist church and its teachings. It really resonated with me, and I became curious. John invited me to go to church with him to meet people, and I fell in love with the community and they took me under their wing with even more teachings. I felt safe there and able to grow in that environment. I believe I chose my family. It hasn't been easy, but I survived, and it helped me with my compassion towards others. I never want anyone to ever feel like I did.

Jacqueline Davis is a spiritual healer, a Reiki 2 practitioner, and a tarot card reader. Her mission is to heal the world by helping one person heal at a time. She has lived in the Boston area for her whole life. The SheBreathes Collaborative community has provided her with guidance and support, for which she's extremely grateful.

Learn more about Jacqueline on Instagram
@jacqueline_psychic_healer

KATHY SLACK

IN SYNC WITH MYSELF:
IN PURSUIT OF ALIGNMENT

My story is about becoming. To some, it may seem obvious, but for me, it was a revelation when I realized that becoming is a lifelong journey. A journey each of us needs to be an active participant in, otherwise what we become will be determined by our circumstances and what others decide we are.

Sadly, I speak of this with firsthand knowledge, because I had become exactly that – defined by the outside expectations of society and others. It took me a long time to realize what the source of the discontentment in my life was. I was always feeling inadequate and insufficient, and I had resigned myself to the fact that that was what I was, inadequate and insufficient. The truth is, outside expectations are fickle and inconsistent, and living up to them is unachievable.

Eventually, I came to realize the reason I was experiencing these feelings of inadequacy was that I had never taken the time to honestly think about what I wanted and what mattered to me personally. Taking the time to sit with myself and do the work of answering those questions, based on my own personal values and perspectives, helped me to source out what my life treasure is and in turn, learn how to pursue it. Now, for the most part, I understand and can voice my reasons why I make the choices I make and what it is I am trying to achieve. And, in those moments when I'm feeling lost or unsure, I can take out my compass and remind myself where I am headed and what it is I am striving for.

The work has not been easy. It has taken strength and courage that I did not know I had, and I often still feel that I don't adequately possess. When I first started this journey, it felt exhilarating to pause and take the time to identify and state for myself what I wanted to accomplish and how I wanted to live. Prior to this, I had never really thought about it; I was just living my life. But now, for more than a decade, perhaps two, I have been doing a deep dive into defining and reevaluating what matters most to me personally and working to live a life that is reflective of those truths. This task is more challenging than it appears. Many times while traveling this path, I have found it very uncomfortable to sit with myself and quite difficult to identify what is truly meaningful to me and what it is I need to do to pursue it.

As each area of importance in my life came to my mind, whether it was relationships with family and friends, being a wife, my parenting, my career, my home, my finances, myself, my hobbies, or my desires, I became painfully aware of how far off I was from where I wanted to be. The pain I encountered in this process took me by surprise. It wasn't identifying the areas of my life that are meaningful that caused me pain, the pain came in realizing just how much of a discrepancy there was in the way I was living my life from what my true heartfelt desires were.

Experiencing this realization brought on an immense flood of emotion and overwhelming feelings of sadness, regret, and fear. My emotional mind reacted to this onslaught with justification, blame, and excuses. These emotional reactions, although self-protective in their own way, were often detrimental and prevented me from moving forward. Throughout my life, it was always my intention to do better; I was just too busy, I thought I was doing the best I could. Truth is, I was always reacting to the environment and needs as they presented themselves to me, and I was never really in control. I wanted that to change. I wanted to be proactive and intentional with my words, actions, and behaviors.

Sadness and regret arose in me with the awareness of all the years and experiences that had passed, everything I couldn't get back or redo. I found it shameful, and I was full of regret that I hadn't taken the time to set my priorities, establish my values, and make a conscious determination to live by them. I mean, they were part of me, always present in my subconscious and influenced my life, but they weren't my guiding force. They were in the background.

Fear set in with the thought that it was too late for me to make these changes. The sense that my behaviors, roles, and relationships had been established and there was no changing, fixing, or improving them made me discouraged. I felt there was a slim chance that I would be successful at making any significant changes or ever fulfilling my hopes and dreams. I had become what I was going to be. My fear was exacerbated by the idea that if I did consider attempting to make changes, it would put me at risk. I felt like my life was in a delicate balance, and any catalyst could make it all fall apart. Relationships might be ruined, I might not achieve my goals, and I could ruin my career in the process of pursuing them. I realize now that a big part of these feelings was due to the fact that I did not have my own firm foundation to work from.

If I'm being honest, there were moments when working to put my life in order would evoke such a strong emotional response that I just needed to stop. The truth was that even though I knew the way I was living wasn't going to lead to achieving my highest desires, potential, and goals, it was familiar and safe. Change is hard and uncomfortable. When things got uncomfortable, I would pause. I would revert to living with the day-to-day needs and experiences of life, and I would feel a sense of relief and safety. I was married, raising three children (the fourth born along the way), working as an RN, maintaining a home, and focusing on family relationships. All this seemed to consume my time, and I could convince myself I was content. A month, six months, a year might pass before I would be willing and ready again to confront the dissatisfaction and discontentment I was feeling. Then, once again, the nagging idea that I needed things to be different would creep back in, and I couldn't ignore it, I would dig back into my self-work. I would be reminded through some circumstance, or maybe several, that although this inner work was painful, it was necessary. I would look again at my notes and journals and redetermine what I wanted in this life, what truly mattered, and begin once again to think about what I needed to do to get there. I would recommit myself to making a priority list of what mattered most to me, and deciding on a plan and a reasonable timeline to accomplish my goals. I worked on my own behavior patterns, did my best to resist reacting to outside expectations and opinions, and worked to learn to say what I truly thought and wanted.

What mattered was that my life wasn't in alignment with what my gold was, and I needed to figure out how to mine for it. The courage and strength to address the areas of my life that were out of alignment came from my faith and spirituality. At the start of this journey, I felt prompted to do this self-work, and I was thoughtful in identifying in specific detail what I wanted to accomplish in my life, what it would look like, and how I would achieve it. My process also involved defining what kind of person I wanted to be, which relationships mattered to me, what my priorities were, and what I needed to do to live by them.

Throughout my life, my relationships have been defined in a certain way. Establishing new boundaries and expectations was terrifying to me; it still is at times. Even identifying my boundaries and expectations for myself has been a challenge, never mind figuring out how to communicate them to others, expect others to respect them, and finally, deciding what I was willing to risk in order to establish them.

I have always listened to the voices of others. And I realized that up to this point, my own voice hadn't been heard, not by me and not by anyone else. Sadly, I didn't expect it to be. And the fact is, if we don't identify an expectation, it can't be met. I began to think about why. Why do I think the way I think? Why do I act the way I act? Why do I do the things I do?

Of course, this led me to thoughts of my childhood experiences and upbringing.

As most of us do, I have often reflected on my childhood. Throughout my childhood and early adult life, I strove to be the person I thought I was expected to be. I do not consider this as negative necessarily. The expectations I perceived included being a good citizen, truthful, kind, generous, loving, and respectful. The problem is, in my mind, I have never lived up to these expectations.

I have also reflected on why I am so uncomfortable asserting my opinion. I suspect it has to do with birth order and chaos and conflict. My mom immigrated from Ireland at 19, met my dad in Boston, and was married at 23. I am the youngest of five children. My siblings are all about a year apart, and I was born five years after the fourth. My mom had some difficulty with childbearing in the years between. My mom always told me I was meant to be born; she was scheduled to have her tubes tied twice before my birth, but due to some unfortunate circumstances for her, the procedure hadn't been performed. Although, in hindsight, it is fortunate for me, because I am here.

The story did make me feel special. I always felt like I had a unique connection with my mom. I suspect that all five of us had that feeling. My mom was a special lady. She arrived in the United States with the equivalent of an 8th-grade education. After raising us, she went to school, obtained her G.E.D., and then went to college and became a registered nurse, working as an RN into her 70s. My dad was a good but difficult man. His behavior was erratic. He was a bit of a tantrum thrower, but he loved and cared for his family as best he knew how. He grew up during the Depression, the second oldest of 15 children and the oldest boy. His dad, my grandfather, died in his 50s, and after that, my father needed to help care for and financially support his family. My dad was a responsible and dependable man. I always knew I could turn to him in need. My family wasn't perfect, and things could have been better. It hurts my heart to critique my parents, because I love them dearly. I know I was more fortunate than many and perhaps less fortunate than others. As a mom myself, the awareness of my own shortcomings and the wishes and lament of "would have, could have, should have" thinking makes me sad. I know I can't rewind the clock, and I wish I did better for my children while they were growing up. And as far as my parents are concerned, what I know for sure is they loved me, and they did their best.

As a child, I was alone a lot. Well maybe not actually alone, but I felt alone. I spent quite a bit of time away from home, either at my friends' houses or at my aunt's house. My aunt and my cousins spent time with me, and I didn't feel alone there. I would stay for weeks at a time and not see my parents or siblings. They were all busy. My mom had been a stay-at-home mom when my siblings were younger, but she went to work when I was about five years old. She worked in the evening, so her hours at home were my hours in school and I missed her a lot. Around the time I was in high school, my mom went back to school to work toward her degree. Interestingly, we ended up in nursing school at the same time. We went to different schools, but we became study buddies, and those are truly precious memories for me.

So perhaps the idea that no one cared what I thought or wanted began in early childhood. But sadly, and probably most important to note, throughout my childhood into adulthood, I was on that list of people who didn't care about what I thought or what I wanted.

I began to wonder: if I didn't care about myself and what I thought or felt, how could I expect others to treat me any other way? I didn't respect my voice. I didn't listen to me. I didn't create boundaries.

Regardless of why I had developed this mindset, I had now identified a core problem and barrier to my ability to achieve the life I longed to live. The next step I faced was figuring out how to change it. As I said, my relationships have been established. My relationship with finances, my roles as daughter, wife, mother, nurse, friend, etc. were already written, and now I wanted to change the script. As far as I could tell, this mostly involved speaking up, setting boundaries, and self-discipline.

I decided to start with the roles and relationships that in my mind would be the easiest to alter and seemed to pose the least risk. I began with my finances and my role in the workplace. Addressing my finances turned into its own deep dive and is ongoing and my struggle with self-discipline is a significant factor. For my role in the workplace, I decided I would define the kind of nurse and employee that I would be, and I decided that my expectations were the expectations I needed to live up to. I resisted the inclination to respond to all the ideas and input from others. Changing my paradigm in that way did not come easy. I was afraid. I thought it would ruin my relationships and make my employment less secure. My identity in part has always involved being agreeable. I felt that agreeableness made me a better nurse, coworker, and employee. The problem was, being too agreeable can lead to erasing your own voice. It was awkward at first when I began to speak up and started to share my honest ideas and opinions. But now I can tell you that I don't even remember how people reacted to me, I just know it felt good and was empowering to honestly express myself. Surprisingly, I felt rejuvenated, and I began to see possibility and potential. Turns out, my standards for me were higher than the ones imposed upon me. I realized I wanted new and different opportunities. I went back to school and began my path to becoming a nurse practitioner and opening my own practice. If I'm being truthful, my comfort is still in agreeableness. I still believe agreeableness is a positive trait and promotes therapeutic relationships, so long as I don't allow it to prevent me from speaking my truth.

Not all the changes I have begun to incorporate have turned out so well. There are habits and behaviors that have proven to be quite difficult to change, and there are several close relationships that ended once I began to express myself more assertively and authentically. I still have moments of wanting to reach out to those individuals and make it OK, but I know that doing so would be a betrayal to myself. I am really working hard not to do that anymore. There are also a few relationships I still don't feel quite ready to take the risk. Perhaps fear is the reason that I am reluctant to address some of my relationships. Fear is a struggle for me. I don't want to betray myself, if I decide I need to set a boundary, I need to also decide what my action will be if it is not honored. I am finding that people are often personally offended when you try to establish new or any boundaries, especially in more longstanding and intimate relationships. Right now, I am working on my relationship with myself, including holding myself accountable to my boundaries, which also intertwines with my relationship with money and finances as well as my tendency to agreeableness.

I have set the intention to not allow myself to treat me any other way than the way I want to be treated (it is a battle).

The initial work of defining my own thoughts, desires, and expectations was key to implementing personal changes with any confidence or conviction. Who is Kathy? What does Kathy want? These were foreign questions to me. Frankly, I feel the self-care phenomenon can border on selfishness at times, and I didn't want to be selfish. I found, and still find, it is uncomfortable for me to focus on myself. But it was in working to answer these questions that I developed a desire and excitement for change. I had identified where my treasure, was and I could now live my life in pursuit of it. The shame and regret I felt for the inability to live up to outside expectations was replaced by a determination to live up to my own expectations.

So, who am, I and what is it that matters to me? Being honest and trustworthy matters. My faith, my children, my family, my home, my profession, my experiences, and my relationships matter. I must stay mindful of the fact that what I have influence and control over is who I am in each of these areas. I am the person I still manage to forget to put on the list of what matters to me. My relationship with myself matters.

Other aspects of my life that are part of this journey so far include myself, my finances, my home, my career, my personal development, goals, interests, and hobbies. I know what I am striving for, and I am realizing that I can make decisions and choices that align with my highest intentions.

I believe we are all uniquely and divinely designed, yet we share common threads that are woven throughout the tapestry of our individual beings. We may not share the exact same struggles, but we learn and grow and are empowered by one another. We are not always aware of how we affect each other, but we can be absolutely confident that we do.

I do not want to end this story by suggesting that I have completed this process. It is ongoing and ever-changing. As my life progresses, what I see as my treasure may change, but now I realize I will decide what that is, and I will continue to pursue it consciously and actively. Forgetting what is behind and straining toward what is ahead, I press on toward the goal.

Kathleen Slack is blessed to be a mom of four amazing individuals, the primary purpose of her life on earth. Identifying and pursuing her own hopes and dreams is part of showing her family that she matters, as every one of us does. Kathy loves the water, visiting family in Ireland, and skiing with family and friends. She's a passionate reader and life-long learner. Kathy believes caring for our mental health can improve our biological, emotional, social, and spiritual well-being. She is an integrative psychiatric nurse practitioner, providing comprehensive and thoughtful care for each client in her practice, Integrative Psychiatry and Wellness. Kathy has worked as a registered nurse for oncology allergy, immunology, and post-partum departments.

She encourages individuals to connect with who they are and strive for their own healing and wholeness, and hopes this story communicates the importance of finding and listening to yourself.

$\mathcal{R}obin$

ROBIN RYAN MARQUEZ

WHAT THE HELL...
WHY CAN'T WE ALL BE WELL?

My story, like many, is one of pain to purpose. It started with my own breast cancer journey in 2005. I was happily married, 42 years old with four children under the age of seven when I was diagnosed with stage two invasive breast cancer. I was a busy working mother, and I thought I was in good physical shape. So, you can imagine my surprise when I was in the shower one day and happened to find a palpable lump the size of a chickpea.

Having worked in the medical field for over two decades as a physical therapist, I certainly appreciated the value of good health. I had always been an athlete in high school and college. I was religious about going to annual wellness appointments and started my breast screening mammograms at the early age of 36 with the belief that early detection is key to treatment. Each year after completing my annual mammogram, I would receive a letter from my doctor stating that everything was normal, except for a notation that I did have small calcifications and extremely dense tissue in both breasts. I always thought this was a good thing, like strong muscles. I immediately went to see my doctor, confused as to why my recent mammogram two months ago did not detect or see anything. My doctor simply wanted to repeat the mammogram in case we missed something.

Once I was in the exam room, the lump in my right breast was clearly visible, so the technician had no problem targeting the radiation to include the lump in the testing area. As I watched the clock tick by, several women came and went, so I asked the receptionist if they had forgotten about me. When the technician returned, she informed me that nothing showed up on the mammogram and stated that my doctor wanted to repeat the mammogram.

Yes, that's right. Two mammograms were performed in one day which showed nothing due to my increased breast density. Mammography for me did not reveal the additional four tumors in my right breast, which were later confirmed with a breast ultrasound and MRI.

I underwent the traditional allopathic treatment model of chemotherapy, surgery for the removal of several lymph nodes, bilateral mastectomies, tissue expanders, and later reconstruction with silicone gel breast implants. My cancer was estrogen-sensitive so I was put on Tamoxifen, a hormone therapy estrogen blocker.

Due to my history of endometriosis and infertility in my 20s and 30s, my medical team determined I was at high risk for uterine cancer and recommended my uterus and ovaries be removed. I thought that made sense. Why risk getting another type of cancer while preventing a recurrence of breast cancer? The following year, I started experiencing pelvic floor issues with vaginal pain, thinning of the tissues, and occasional incontinence, which then led to additional surgery for a bladder sling.

Initially, I went for eight weeks of physical therapy, which helped me regain my endurance, range of motion, and strength in my shoulders and arms, but it did nothing to address the restrictions and pain from my surgical scars. I was never referred to a pelvic floor therapist to address weak pelvic floor muscles that were contributing to urinary leakage, thinning, and atrophy of vaginal tissue, all a result of being thrown into Menopause at age 43, thanks to chemotherapy and Tamoxifen.

I remember the day my oncologist declared I had no evidence of disease (NED) from the cancer, which basically means you are in remission. I should have been thrilled, right? Well, not exactly. Why did I still have all these side effects and issues? Why did no one offer any help?

I remember asking my doctor if I could get a referral for a pelvic floor physical therapist, and he half-jokingly said, "You're a physical therapist. Can't you do your own therapy?"

What the heck? I felt like saying, "Do cardiac surgeons do their own open-heart surgery?"

Even though I had been a therapist for many years, when I got cancer, I had never worked in the field of oncology. As a matter of fact, that was the furthest thing from my mind. I thought cancer care was depressing! Clearly, the Universe had a different plan for me.

It was my own need to find solutions and treatments for the side effects I was facing which affected my daily quality of living, my relationships, and my self-esteem. This was the driving force for me to take many hours of additional educational training in order to specialize in oncology rehabilitation. I sought out mentors to learn more for my personal benefit but also to offer other women solutions for the problems I was experiencing. I became certified in myofascial release, manual lymphatic drainage, and pelvic floor rehab. I then started working in my mentor's private practice part-time while I was practicing my newly acquired skills. I would then cover for her full-time when she went on vacation. That soon became three months out of the year.

The next big leap of faith came when my mentor decided to retire and sell her practice. It was then that I decided to dive deep into the world of oncology rehab full-time.

If anyone ever tells you being an entrepreneur and owning your own practice is easy, then they probably haven't done it. Even though I had worked within this practice for five years before I bought it, I still had no idea of what I was getting myself into.

In 2017, approximately one year prior to purchasing the practice, I underwent what I thought was going to be a relatively easy procedure to have my implants replaced, because it had been more than ten years and my plastic doctor recommended exchanging them for a new set to decrease my risk of having them rupture or leak. This made sense, and I certainly didn't want to risk silicone leaking into my body. But looking back, I didn't know that the medical field had not yet perfected the surgical unblock technique, where the whole breast capsule is removed when taking out breast implants. The reason for this is to contain any heavy metals and toxins stored within the capsule or breast implant that could be released. What I later learned after reading the post-operative report was that extensive scarring of my muscles on my chest wall limited doctors from completely removing the capsules. Instead, the breast capsules were left in place and cross-hatched to get more expansion of tissue but this merely released a bunch of toxins into my chest cavity before they inserted the new implants and closed me up.

Initially, I healed without any significant difficulties. It took a few weeks and some soft tissue work on my breast scars to regain my range of motion and my strength, but it was not as challenging a time as my original surgery. I was back to work in four weeks and managed to resume treating my oncology patients. My body probably could have used a few more weeks to recover, but I felt guilty leaving my clients without care for such an extended period. So, I ignored the painful daily messages my body was sending me to slow down and take it easy. Once I officially purchased the practice, it was full steam ahead!

Most of the existing clients continued when my mentor retired, and therefore I had an immediate caseload of patients and no shortage of work. The business was successful and moving right along the first year. I was exhausted, and I no longer had enough time to engage in my normal health routines, so they were put on hold.

What free time I did have, my husband and I were helping

to manage our four young adults, all in college at once at that point. That's a lot of moving in and out of dorms and parent weekend events, visits, etc.

It was during this time that my mother's health also began to show signs of aging. She and I were very close, and she was a key role model in my life as well as my children's lives. She had always been an amazingly strong and independent working woman, a social worker who lived many years alone after my dad passed away. She worked with clients until she was 75. But we started to notice she was having more falls and difficulties with short-term memory loss. Initially, she was able to conceal this quite well. Eventually, one fall too many landed her in the hospital. It was determined at age 80 that she was no longer able to live alone without home services. She had always agreed that when the time came, she would allow home care services to assist her in her health needs, but this was not the case. She refused, not realizing the significance of her short-term memory loss, and was not agreeable to moving into an assisted living facility, so I had to acquire guardianship to help manage her healthcare and safety. This was probably one of the hardest things I have ever had to do, and it broke my heart. She had always found the time and space to take care of me and my family while I was going through cancer, surgeries, and recoveries over the years, and now the roles were reversing. Now I was the caregiver and she was the one needing the assistance, and that was challenging. I think part of me felt betrayed and angry that she did not keep up her end of the agreement to let home services help her when she needed it most.

It was determined that an assisted living facility close to my home would be the best option so I could visit frequently. Over the next few years, my health began to deteriorate. I continued to work, but I was exhausted most of the time. Between taking care of my family, work, and now being the healthcare proxy and guardian of my mother, I had no time for myself, and I lost my own identity. I was just surviving clearly not thriving.

I had developed a list of new symptoms that seemed to pop up daily, such as corneal neuropathy, eye pain, headaches, joint pain, decreased energy, and shortness of breath.

My heavy metals, liver enzymes, and breast cancer markers were progressively going up, and all my oncologist wanted to do were liver and lymph node biopsies and possibly start chemotherapy if we couldn't get things under control.

Then Covid-19 hit in full swing, and I was forced to close my oncology practice for nine months. This was a blessing for me. Perhaps it was the Universe allowing me the time, space, and energy to address my own health needs I had been ignoring for years now while putting everyone else's first. During this time, I had the opportunity to travel to Hope4Cancer in Tijuana, Mexico; I went with one of my clients as her caregiver.

I read somewhere that successful people have several things in common, among them that they trust their intuition, have patience and faith, and take action. I started to keep a journal before my first trip to Mexico and wrote down anything that came to mind that felt good and that I could see myself doing. No surprise, a major theme emerged around my passion for helping others, particularly educating women about alternative screening and treatment options to biohack the body and activate energy pathways and systems to either upregulate or downregulate DNA genes to work efficiently to achieve optimal health. I kept at it, searching for the idea of what that might look like.

Then one day, I found myself flying in first class with my entire row empty and my client Dorothy sitting in the aisle seat across from me with her row empty as well. As a matter of fact, there were only 25 people, including the flight attendants, on our flight heading to Mexico. It was surreal.

It was then that I noticed the expression on her face, one of great sadness and despair. I also noticed above her masked face a small tear in the corner of her right eye. I asked, "Dorothy, what's wrong?" She looked at me with great intensity and asked, "Why can't we all be well?"

To this, I had no answer, but you can be sure that I pondered that question for the remainder of the flight. You see, my client was diagnosed with stage four metastatic breast cancer in 2005, the same year as myself — coincidentally, or maybe the Universe put the two of us together to learn from one another. I would describe my client and new friend as a seventy-seven-year-young woman, living an extremely active, healthy, vegan lifestyle and in the final stages of finishing her book when cancer reared its ugly head and returned to her lower back and hips. Approximately six months prior to our trip, we met at a rebounding instructor training class. A rebounder is similar to a mini trampoline. I personally found rebounding to be very helpful in regaining my endurance and strength when recovering from chemo fatigue. If used during chemotherapy, rebounding supports the lymphatic system and increases white blood cell formation.

While in Mexico at Hope4Cancer, I decided to have a full evaluation and workup for myself. Having worked in the oncology world for ten years, I knew how the system worked. I had applied for a long-term care health insurance policy literally weeks before I originally got diagnosed with breast cancer. Once my medical record indicated a diagnosis of breast cancer, I had to wait five years after being declared in remission before I was able to get a policy in place. This time I wasn't about to lose my coverage with a second diagnosis of cancer in the States. Thermography and ultrasound testing revealed several enlarged lymph nodes in both the axilla and thyroid. This, in conjunction with my lab reports which confirmed extremely high cancer markers and liver enzymes eight times the normal level, helped the doctors finally connect the dots, and they diagnosed me with breast implant illness with localized cancer in my lymph nodes. I opted to treat without doing any biopsy for risk of spreading the cancer. This time, I chose to treat the localized cancer with all-alternative therapies, including high-dose IV therapy, mistletoe injections, infra-red sauna, Pulsed Electromagnetic Frequencies(PEMF), coffee enemas, an organic plant-based diet, gluten, dairy, sugar, and ETOH-free diet, supplements, and daily exercise. This included five additional trips to Mexico to carry out a detox/RX program over a six-month period. We needed to prepare my body by reducing the burden of cancer and preparing for explant surgery to remove implants/capsules and additional reconstruction of pectoral and intercostal muscles. I made several additional trips to Mexico following explant surgery in order to continue the detoxification of toxins and heavy metals within my chest.

It was during this time that I definitely experienced imposter syndrome – feelings of guilt, shame, and not being good enough. This prevented me from sharing a lot of my own experiences with my patients when I returned to work. There were lots of things I should or could have done better to have prevented getting cancer again.

Being vulnerable with my patients was somehow admitting I had failed at managing my own cancer. It's like going to a trainer who doesn't work out. I thought, who wants to go to a cancer coach with cancer? What I realized was it was the opposite.

I merely shared that I did things completely differently the second time around, and I was able to find treatments to put my cancer back into remission without side effects. I didn't lose my hair and didn't have to undergo any additional surgeries or take pharmaceuticals to manage my pain. I let them know there were multiple ways to improve their health and at the same time feel good, keep working, and do the things they loved.

I found that being authentic and delivering my message from the heart made me more relatable. I asked my patients questions about their breast and pelvic health and how these two areas may be affecting their self-esteem and relationships. A few clients shared that it was the first time in their healing journey that anyone ever asked them about their quality of life. Many medical personnel were only concerned with managing cancer, and the pain, trading one side effect for another without really exploring the root cause of why the patient got cancer or sick in the first place.

During my first cancer journey, I focused on the physical healing and restoration of the body. I have always believed in a higher power and God, but I always imagined it as external to my body. My recent transformation gave me an awakened consciousness to realize that the power that made my body can also help to heal my body.

I did nothing to address the spiritual and emotional components that allowed cancer to develop, therefore, it wasn't surprising that the cancer returned. I was still holding onto anger, guilt, and shame. I never blamed God, but I had not yet forgiven myself. My faith and hope have always been strong. I can honestly say my second diagnosis of cancer did not bring the same degree of fear as the first time.

Cancer taught me several valuable lessons:

CARE FOR MYSELF FIRST

One of the most valuable things my therapist had me do was to make a list of all the people I feel responsible for caring for. She then reminded me to put my name on the list as well. She proceeded to tell me that I was the most important person I would ever care for by saying, "Remember you have the honor to have this highest responsibility of caring for yourself."

She then told me as I moved through my month, to stay true to the role of caregiver, but to keep myself at the forefront as I care for the others I love. I always try to remember this, because the extent to which you rest and care for yourself is directly related to the meaning that your life has, the impact that you will make, and the energy and enthusiasm that you present to the world!

GOOD ENOUGH VS. PERFECTION

I now strive for good enough. Perfection is overrated, and it eliminates your ability to rest. I know I will never attain perfection, and good enough allows me the space to rest. I give my best in every moment or situation, knowing that my best might change in different circumstances or with different people.

"There is a virtue in work and there is a virtue in rest. Use both and overlook neither." – Alan Cohen

I ACCEPT ME

I am perfectly imperfect. My flaws create the beautiful tapestry of my being. As I grow and change, I am becoming more of who I am meant to be. I found myself going through a grieving process over the loss of my breasts, uterus, and ovaries, and again when my implants were removed. Initially, I felt disconnected from my body and my divine feminine power of intuition. It took time and both physical and mental work to reconnect and realize that the loss of body parts is not what defines me as a woman. We all can tap into our inner energy, which remains with or without our body parts. I also now realize my divine feminine power comes from within. I no longer look for approvals from external sources. It took time for me to realize that how I feel about my body is not about what others think, but more about how I feel about myself and what stories hold true for me. My scars now represent a new sense of power, growth, and transformation.

I REALIZE I AM ENOUGH

Being trained with a medical/science education, I always thought I had to look outside of myself for the answers. However, I now realize that all I ever need is within me, including a conscious-logical mind and a caring heart. I think it was

Maya Angelou who once said (and I'm paraphrasing), "Why is it that we can all delight in the beauty of a butterfly, but we rarely take the time to contemplate the challenges it had to go through to achieve that beauty?"

I GO AT MY SPEED

I am not timing myself. It doesn't matter how slowly I move. As long as I move every day in a purposeful forward movement, I am proud of my progress. My speed is enough. I am exactly where I need to be. I can now say yes to my pace and not have to keep up with others. This year will be my 10th year hiking Mount Washington (elevation 6,288 ft) in New Hampshire as a fundraiser for Breast Cancer Peaks for Prevention, which has raised almost a million dollars with a small group of dedicated volunteers. Every year, my goal is to complete the hike with no injuries. I may not be the first person up the mountain, but I'm not the last, and that's just fine with me!

I CAN MAKE CHOICES

I realize I can make different choices in the process of what I am creating or manifesting. I can shift my thoughts and reactions to situations by meditating, praying, deciding who I spend my time with, and avoiding negative conversations or interactions. When we choose to think, believe, and act from a position of power, refusing to be a victim of circumstances, then the healer within automatically strengthens. When we refuse to live under the influence of worry and doubt, then our internal life force is enriched and empowered.

WHEN HEALING INCLUDES PASSAGE FROM THIS LIFE

This is one of the most extraordinary lessons I have learned in over thirty years of medical practice. This is usually taught by a person experiencing a severe or terminal disease. It's not guaranteed that a person who lives the longest is the winner of the game of life. There are unsurvivors who passed away without suffering.

It would be remiss of me to complete my story without mentioning the lesson my friend taught me. Now she will give this teaching to you as well: surrendering to death is also a self-healing practice.

Dorothy had used health enhancement and self-healing methods in many forms throughout her life. She was a community-minded person, not someone who seemed likely to "die before her time." Being a health educator and spiritual seeker did not spare her from breast cancer, which eventually metastasized to the bone. Ultimately, she came to realize that her departure from this life was inevitable.

Over the years, Dorothy had developed her own personal approach to the practice of self-healing. Now she purposefully turned her intention toward a kind of euthanasia in which self-healing became part of her life completion process. She had support from hospice workers, a network of devoted family and friends, and expert medical assistance. She added to self-healing methods by deepening her spiritual practice. When she realized that her resistance to losing her life was draining her vitality and making her condition worse, her faith expanded, and she began to surrender. This led to the essence of forgiveness: forgiving oneself. She became calm, like a wisdom teacher. People commented that she was beginning to look radiant, with a sparkle in her eye.

When it became impossible for her to continue the movement

practices, she used breath practice, deep relaxation, and meditation. When she could no longer massage herself, she received massages from family and friends.

Dorothy taught many people a powerful lesson on how peaceful leaving this life can be. Because of her wisdom, her practice of self-healing included faith, forgiveness, and surrender. She left a great message for her family and friends: death is not frightening or unkind. Genuine healing doesn't ask that we cheat death; it asks only that we live honestly.

MY FINAL REFLECTION

I've always felt a sense of urgency to share my learned wisdom with other women about alternative screening options like thermography, especially for women with dense breasts. I'm so passionate about this because I believe this is what saved my life — detecting my cancer the second time when it was in the earliest stages and had only spread locally to lymph nodes/thyroid rather than waiting for additional tumors to develop or taking biopsies and risking spreading the cancer.

I started listening to my own intuition telling me what my body really needed and what was not serving me. I was then able to let go of all of the roles I thought I had to play and the limiting beliefs I held about my own guilt and self-worth as a woman. It's more about feeling comfortable in your own body. Being a woman is not about the sum of your body parts. There are many women who have beautiful, imperfect bodies with all the working parts but feel completely disassociated with their bodies, energy, and inner wisdom.

I now realize that maintaining good health is a choice and a lifetime process. It changes as we age and become more connected to our inner wisdom, and we are better able to find the answers within us if we slow down, get quiet, and listen to the messages the body is sending.

I stand for the possibility of divine intuition, health, and love for all, which brings me back to my friend's question that I have thought about for years:

Why can't we all be well?

This one question is the reason I founded the nonprofit, Wings To Health, Inc.

WTH stands for both Wings To Health and What The Hell, Why Can't We All Be Well!!

Our mission is to offer physical, emotional, and spiritual wellness while incorporating various modalities to assist with the side effects of treatment, body restoration, pain management, education, and more. We share knowledge for wellness with younger women and those less fortunate to arm them with skills to lead a healthy illness-free lifestyle well into the future.

WTH refers to outside services for further follow-up, aligning with organizations in the community that share a similar mission.

Robin Ryan Marquez is a licensed Physical Therapist with 30+ years in practice.

Her life's work is devoted to dramatically shifting the women's health movement to ensure that every woman has access to the full spectrum of healing, support, and services she deserves for both preventative and palliative care.

Her personal experience as a survivor of recurring breast cancer had everything to do with her wanting to help other women better navigate their journey back to wellness. Traditional therapies left her with many limitations relating to range of motion, pain, and pelvic floor dysfunction. Her personal drive led her to seek out and explore alternative treatments not offered by the traditional medical world.

Motivated to share her knowledge with others, she set out on her soul's mission to help other women navigate their healing journey and obtain optimal wellness.

To learn more about Robin, visit her at www.circleofwellnessforwomen.com

Christel

CHRISTEL POIRIER

THE JOURNEY OF AN ALCHEMIST

It was two weeks before Christmas, my favorite holiday. I was only 15 and could never have imagined the direction my life was about to take. There was a chill in the air, so I wore my gloves on that frigid day when I left my house...never to return.

The next moment that I'd remember was slowly opening my eyes, one week later, from what would remain a long-distance memory. I had just awoken from a coma. I was in the ICU, severely injured from being a passenger in a horrific car accident, with friends, on the way to a holiday party. I was unconscious at the scene and was rescued by the "jaws of life" in order to be removed from the vehicle. I was then air-lifted by helicopter, to a Boston hospital. Having suffered severe head trauma, I had fallen into a coma.

My arm was severely injured, with a limited range of motion and stuck at a ninety-degree angle. My elbow was dislocated, my wrist had suffered a fracture. And my foot was deeply cut. When I awoke to the traumatic reality, I felt tremendous pain as I lay there motionless. I was comforted by my beautiful mother's voice. She was by my side and took my hand in hers. I was overcome with emotion. I listened as she comforted me, explaining where I was and what had happened.

I then heard a nurse gently whisper to my mother, "It's OK, take your time." And, then, for a moment, she held my hand a little tighter and said, "I have to tell you something.... The house burned down last night."

I could not believe what I heard. But I'll never forget what she said.

Despite being disoriented. I felt overwhelmed with emotion. I couldn't find a reality to hold onto and was drifting in and out of consciousness.

I had just awoken from a coma to hear that our home was gone. We lost everything in the fire. Our personal belongings, our family photos, and childhood keepsakes. All gone. In that tragic moment, I felt like all that was left was just a shell of me.

My mother later shared that my grandmother (her mother), who lived upstairs from us, had suffered smoke inhalation and had been transported to a different Boston hospital. My mother had endured so much. She was told by the doctors that it was unlikely I would survive the accident, as they handed her the jewelry I had worn that day. They explained that if I did survive, it wasn't likely that I would walk or talk again. Then, just one week following the accident, she watched in horror as my grandmother collapsed in the fire while attempting to be rescued. And then she'd witnessed our home and everything in it burn to the ground.

My mother was an extremely strong woman who learned even greater strength and faith during this time. My mother prayed for our recovery. My grandmother did fully recover soon after and was discharged from the hospital.

I was later transferred to another hospital for rehabilitation. It was there that I worked with both speech therapists and physical therapists. I was determined to learn to walk and talk again.

I continued with my therapies. Some days were better than others. I will never forget the day that I took my first steps forward. It was challenging, to say the least. But, with great will, I was determined and continued working at it, every day. Some days, only a half step. And others, a baby step. But, forward movement, nonetheless. I was making great progress with every step.

Every step, whether big or small, is an integral part of your journey — it's with every step and all of the moments in between that we pave the path of our experience. And in every moment, we have a choice. I made my choice. I was determined to walk again. And, one fine day, with one foot in front of the other, I took a brave step forward. And, then another. That was the day I began to walk again. What an incredible moment that was. That accomplishment made such a powerful impact, and it greatly influenced my ability to focus my intention on healing. I could feel in every fiber of my being, that I would make it through this.

"*You must find the place inside yourself where nothing is impossible.*" — Deepak Chopra

With both feet on the ground, I continued to move forward. I had simultaneously been meeting with speech therapy. We began our work together by creating sounds. We then continued using each sound to create words. At first, it was very challenging. Within the silence, I once again felt an overwhelming energy of freedom from the current limitations that I had faced. And, in that moment, I knew that I would overcome this. When I did speak, it would be life-changing. One of the first things I said was to my mother. I told her that I met with my grandfather (her father) while I was in the coma. He had crossed over two years prior. My loving grandfather came to me like a guiding light, comforted me, and told me that everything was going to be okay. It wasn't my time. We communicated through love. I was in my heart and out of my body. My spirit filled with comfort, peace, and the purest love. It was an extraordinary experience.

From that point forward, my life had changed. This was the beginning of a spiritual awakening . I was deeply connected with spirit and continued to be divinely guided.

My mindset shifted in many ways. For one thing, I realized that despite being in the midst of tragedy and having suffered severe trauma and tremendous loss, on many levels, I had gained such an awareness in that moment.

Although this horror had happened, I was alive. My family survived the fire and I survived the accident. I didn't lose "everything;" I had everything. I had my family, and I had my life. I was blessed to continue on my journey. I knew that I had a profound purpose.

At 15, in that moment, I understood what was truly valuable.

It is not material things. And, when you have nothing tangible and you focus instead on love and healing, peace and gratitude, you have everything, and so much more. It is a whole other world.

"If everything around you seems dark, look again, you may be the light." — Rumi

I was eventually discharged from the rehabilitation hospital, with doctor's orders to return home, while maintaining outpatient speech and physical therapy.

I didn't have a home to return to. My family was invited to stay with my beautiful aunt. She was my favorite aunt, an amazing soul who would give the shirt off her back to help anyone. And she did.

At that time, her home was very small, with one bedroom and one bathroom. There were six of us living together in this small space. But, it was amazing. We had shelter, we had family... and we had a Christmas tree! It was days before Christmas. And, it would be a Christmas like no other. Traditionally, our family's Christmases were out of a storybook, beautiful — with the halls decked, the tree twinkling magic, eggnog, spiced treats, gifts wrapped in big bows, and heartfelt celebrations for days!

This year was different. And, it was special. We may not have shared the same tradition that year. But, we started a new one.

I remembered sitting on the loveseat in my aunt's living room, gazing at the Christmas tree. I couldn't move around easily and would have much time to sit and reflect. I realized the amount of love that I felt in that "small" space, with my beautiful family. In that space of loss, in that space of grief, I felt an abundance of gratitude.

And, born from that moment became one of my mother's and my favorite sayings: "It's the little things in life." All of the little things. The small moments... listening to your favorite song, the comfort of a loving voice, a smile, a hug, compassion from a warm heart, warm gloves, a soft blanket, a glimmer of hope, a moment of peace.

And with this awareness, I found the ability to maintain a positive spirit above any physical circumstance – to transform the horror into wisdom, and the pain into strength. This would become a great catalyst for my healing and growth.

"*Alchemy is the art of turning the lead of our lives into the gold of our dreams.*" – Terence McKenna

I spent my time reading books on holistic health and healing practices. I always had a great interest in meditation and connecting with spirit, prior to the accident. But, it became my practice thereafter. About six months later, I no longer needed speech therapy. I was speaking as if nothing had ever happened.

One year later, after continuing my journey with physical therapy, I had made a full recovery. I could walk again, as I always had. And I regained full range of motion and could completely straighten my arm again. I focused on my studies and was home-schooled for the remainder of the year. I later attended both afternoon and evening classes to obtain the credits required, and then graduated with my class.

I continued to develop my intuition and continued on my healing journey. I felt very blessed to have survived the accident, and it awakened me to a deeper meaning in my life. My journey was unique. I didn't share the traditional high school experience. Not only was I home-schooled for the majority of the time, but this time was dedicated to healing. Which allowed for more meaningful time and connection with my closest family. For this, I am eternally grateful.

I found peace and inspiration through meditation, music, and art, which would all become an integral part of my life.

From a young age, I loved art, music, singing, and dancing. I began painting and writing from a young age. I danced competitively from the age of five until about the age of 12. I always enjoyed singing from the moment I learned I had a voice. Later, I went on to sing with bands. I was asked to sing backup vocals on an album for a band that had previously cast me in some of their music videos. I remember recording in the music studio and being completely in my element.

Music is one of the fastest ways to shift your vibration. I worked closely with this modality. I continued on this path and became an actress, another life-long dream. I was cast in over a dozen Hollywood feature films, music videos, and commercials. I worked alongside some of my favorite actors and actresses and realized that I was living in alignment with my passions and dreams.

Despite being told I wasn't going to make it — not just by the doctors, but by naysayers alike — I kept going. I transmuted all of the pain I had endured, pouring that energy into my creativity, my soul desires, my gifts, and my passions.

THE JOURNEY OF AN ALCHEMIST

With all of that focused intention and belief, I continued on a golden path to manifest my dreams. With each experience, my journey was enriched. I continued to come into greater alignment with my core soul purpose. This in itself provided an abundance of healing to my soul.

"The Universe is responding to your vibration, not to your words or your action." — Abraham Hicks

We all have a purpose and our own unique gifts. The journey of discovering them is where the magic happens. It is in the becoming. The space in between, that's where the gold is, within these spaces. For me, in spaces of great pain, I've learned wisdom. Through spaces of deep grief was born great strength. And through the tragedy of loss, I found gratitude and self-love.

Like the moon, we must go through phases of emptiness to feel full again. And, through these transformative experiences, I did.

I have gone on to meet many interesting and talented people. I've had unforgettable conversations and experiences that I will forever cherish. I have always been an artist. At this point in my journey, these were the places where I had focused my artistic expression most.

Through art, music, and acting, I was experiencing great joy, healing, and soul resonance. I felt aligned with the energies around me and continued to dive deeper into this experience. I realized something very important. I had manifested my healing experience, which would take me to a greater destination.

"The meaning of life is to find your gift. The purpose of life is to give it away." — Pablo Picasso

That is exactly what I set out to do.

I felt inspired to continue on a healing path to share my gifts with the world. I had known I was an old soul from a very young age.

I was often described by others as being wise beyond my years, and sensitive to the energies around me since childhood. However, after surviving the accident, and having gone through an out-of-body experience, my sensitivity to energy and spirit increased.

I studied with Masters and further developed my gifts as a healer. I connected deeply with my intuition, and my connection with spirit was strengthened. I began receiving Reiki attunements, which led me to becoming a Reiki Master Teacher. I immersed myself, wholeheartedly, in healing my mind, body, and soul.

I found great honor in being a source of healing and inspiration to others. I further developed my healing practice and studied holistic health, developing a greater awareness of the importance of listening to your body, honoring your intuition, and healing yourself naturally. After obtaining my certification as a Holistic Health Practitioner, I opened my practice, offering Integrative Energy Healing, Spiritual Healing, and plant-based organic healing products and remedies.

My journey continued down the golden path to manifesting my dreams.

In everything we go through, I believe there is a Divine purpose that is instrumental to our spiritual evolution and personal expansion.

I want the world to know that you all have wisdom, magic, and medicine inside of you. You have the power to heal and transform your life. You are the creator of your own reality. Your past does not determine your future.

And You, Beautiful Soul, Are Enough!

Christel Poirier is a passionate Artist, Actress, Singer, and Healer. As a compassionate and grounded Healer, Christel Poirier is committed to the path of light and transformation. She is a Holistic Health Practitioner, Reiki Master Teacher, Spirit Medium, Angel Messenger Practitioner, and Intuitive Artist.

With great passion, Christel is dedicated to offering spiritual guidance, wisdom, and deep transformational healing to assist others in living their greatest life, by healing themselves naturally, aligning with their core soul purpose, and connecting with their divine blueprint. She is passionate about her healing work with her clients and is dedicated to bringing to them all that is of their highest and best good and assisting them with healing on every level. Christel is the owner of Shangri-La Divine Healing Boutique, where she offers Spiritual and Energy healing, beautifully handcrafted unique gifts, and plant-based organic healing products, each infused with Reiki Energy and conscious intention.

You can learn more about Christel at: *www.shangriladivineboutique.com*

ROBIN PAWLAK GARSTKA

GO LIVE LIFE: A STORY OF SURVIVING TO LIVING

"I'm sorry to have to share this news with you, but it's cancer," my doctor told me.

It was a beautiful autumn afternoon in New England. The leaves on the trees outside were transforming from green to intense shades of gold, orange, and red, and the change of season was in the air. I was sitting in front of my computer at the kitchen counter, as I did most weekdays. Both my teenage boys were in school, and the house was quiet. After waiting several incredibly long days to receive the results of my biopsy, I was somehow startled when the phone rang. I saw the hospital's number. I hesitated to pick up the phone. My body trembled, instinctually knowing the news I was about to hear would not be good.

With a compassionate tone to her voice, my doctor shared the results. Invasive lobular carcinoma. Big words that meant breast cancer. Shit.

She told me my next steps while I scribbled a few details on paper and hung up the phone. I felt numb. At that moment, my life changed forever.

LESSONS ARE IN THE STRUGGLES

You've probably heard the overused catchphrase, "The struggle is real." Those periods of intense and gripping feelings of stress and overwhelm in your life are real. And if the reasons for the struggle are not identified and worked through, they come back like an annoying, stubborn rash that never completely disappears.

The truth is, we all have hardships to overcome, and no one gets a pass. It's inevitable that we will all face difficult days. Struggles are lessons to be learned, self-discoveries unique to each of us. The way we navigate the darkest of times often determines how we see the light again.

At 53, I can see my life like chapters in a book. Chapter one included navigating learning disabilities in school; Chapter two, the inevitable teen heartbreak. Then there are the chapters that include the deaths of close family members, an ADHD and depression diagnosis, a difficult divorce, forced to sell our family home, the loss of jobs, raising two young boys as a single mom with never enough money, and now this chapter. Cancer.

Although my story is filled with challenges, there are also many beautiful moments, laughter, and triumphs. As I turn back the pages now, I can see that each chapter prepared me for the next.

Breast cancer wasn't a new concept to me and my family. My Aunt Leah was 38 when she was first diagnosed. She fought a long, hard battle before dying 10 years later. My grandmother, Martha, was diagnosed at 60 and died at 65. My two great-aunts battled it, too. So I knew the disease was woven into my genes, but the knowing stays somewhere far in the back of your mind while you live. Until it can't stay there anymore. Now it was real for me, too.

REALITY SETTLES IN

A few days after my diagnosis, my oldest son, Quin, turned 18. As we have for so many years, we gathered as a family at our house to celebrate the day he was born, but something was different about this birthday celebration than years past. We all seemed a little more connected, more present with one another. I felt the love that day and the gratefulness we all shared to have this time together.

We have never been a photo-taking family. Many of us are shy around the camera. Maybe it's the extra pounds we have put on over the years, or the way our eyes always seem to squint or blink at the wrong time, but typically we freeze at the words, "Say cheeeeese!" But on this day, we were all in agreement, we needed a photo together.

I ran next door to my neighbor's house and asked if they would mind taking the photo. Then I herded everyone together, and we fell into place in front of the black-framed doorway to my home. With our arms around one another, smiles bright with purpose, I began to think, How many celebrations like this do I have left? Will I get to see my boys become men? Will I know my grandchildren? Will I retire to that dream lake house, where I would hold hands on a porch swing with the love of my life?

It took everything I had to get my health insurance worked out, doctor's appointments lined up, and a surgery date for the mastectomy in the books. I scrambled to learn all I could about my body. I joined a Facebook support group and started seeing a breast cancer specialist to help me navigate the life changes I would need to make.

Over time, the numbness wore off and a reluctant kind of acceptance moved in. I noticed a shift beginning to happen. Every encounter I had with others felt different. Memories came back to me so vividly. People I hadn't seen in a long time came back into my life. Sometimes they would appear physically, and sometimes in my dreams. Places I had been and past experiences would pop into my recollection as clearly as if it were yesterday. I was involuntarily going down memory lane. It was as if the past was trying to tell me something. It felt like I was being forced back through the pages of my life so that I could see what I needed to learn.

THE POWER OF THE INNER GUIDE

I am the youngest of three girls in my family. My sisters Karen and Biz were close in age. I was several years younger and always felt never good enough. I was the one who didn't know how to tie her own shoes, the one who was always screwing up. I was the one who wasn't smart.

Looking back at those years, I see a lot of shame and constant struggle to prove myself. My father grew up at a time when learning disabilities were often seen as laziness and trouble, so he had little patience with me.

Family and friends would laugh at me when I didn't understand something, and school was no better. I remember hearing the word "stupid" a lot. So I started to laugh at myself, too. That made life bearable. I didn't realize it then, but by laughing at myself, I gave everyone permission to continue to laugh at me.

As difficult as my feelings of inadequacy were, I somehow believed I was going to be okay and that I would find my own success someday. It was a voice inside me, just beneath the surface, and it spoke clearly. I knew where my strength was, and that was in art. Time stood still when I worked on anything with my hands. Whether it was drawing, painting, exploring nature, woodworking projects with my father, or simply playing in the mud, creating was in my soul, and I knew that for as long as I can remember.

It's no surprise that when it was time to choose a career path, I decided to go to art school. Shortly after graduation, I landed my first job as a graphic designer at a small design studio in Boston. As a kinesthetic learner, I picked things up quickly, gravitating toward technology. I had found a career path that aligned with my true self and it was empowering.

IDENTIFYING THE PATTERNS OF STRUGGLE

Although my career was going in the right direction, I would still struggle with feelings of inadequacy and shame. I felt stuck, and the stress of that was felt every day. I wasn't truly happy. I couldn't put my finger on it, but I knew I needed help. After a few months of therapy, I was tested and diagnosed with ADHD and depression. Having an ADHD brain can be an intense struggle with equal parts frustration, guilt, overwhelm, and embarrassment, which can lead to depression.

Digging my heels in and researching all I could about my diagnosis gave me great strength. I slowly began to make changes. I started taking medication to help me focus and to lift the fog that had been paralyzing me for so long. Taking action was a pivotal contributor to feeling unstuck. In time, I built up my confidence again and decided to take a leap of faith. I left my full-time job to start a freelance design business, earning several repeat clients that kept me very busy. I began to finally feel the success I yearned for.

I've learned that when my life is moving forward in a positive direction, feelings of overwhelm subside and my depression isn't there, but as soon as I hit another bumpy phase, the same doom and gloom emerges like a dark ghost from its grave, and again, I get stuck.

This pattern has repeated throughout my life and has held me back until I tap into my inner guide and get back on track. Sometimes that has taken only weeks. Sometimes months. Occasionally years.

SILENCING THE INNER VOICE

In my late 20s, life was going well. My boyfriend and I moved into a small two-bedroom apartment on a quiet street in a village outside of Boston. We had known each other for over a year, and we had been talking about marriage. The moment I met him, I knew I would marry him. It was an inner instinct that spoke to me that I can still remember so clearly today. I was 29 and had dated others, but this relationship was different. We were in love and had so much fun traveling to far-away places and exploring new activities together.

When it was time for another adventure, we chose a location we had both not been to before — Key West. We looked forward to the trip for months, planning out every detail.

It was a late morning in November when our trip began. We were rushing around trying to get packed and out the door to the airport when we realized, we couldn't find the plane tickets. While my boyfriend was upstairs looking through drawers and piles of papers, he yelled down to me to check the front pocket of his backpack sitting on the floor in the living room. I unzipped the first pocket I could see. I peeked in and at the same time, my hand reached to the bottom and pulled out a small padded box. Before I could think, my voice inside me said the words "Oh fuck!" I never opened the box that day, but I had a feeling that inside that box was a ring, and I was going to be proposed to in the next few days. I quickly put the box back and opened a different zipper, pulled out the two tickets, and we were off to the airport.

For the hours and days that followed that discovery, my mind went wild. "This is what I had wanted, right? This was the plan, so why was I hesitating? I'm just scared of change, right?"

ACCEPTING LIFE'S PATH

Ignoring my hesitation was the beginning of a long struggle of an emotional decline. Fifteen years after the trip, I found myself a divorced, stressed-out, full-time single mother with two young boys. The marriage was an uphill battle for both of us that left me very depleted and with a loss of my self-worth and drive.

The years following the divorce have required me to turn my own needs off and make decisions that are best for my boys. I love them so much and wouldn't have it any other way.

Looking back with new eyes (thank you, cancer!), I can see

that this was a life lesson meant for me to learn from. In the back of my mind then, I had known instinctually that this would be my journey, which is why I believe I never took action on my doubts and accepted my path.

Accepting your life's path and identifying the lesson is essential to moving forward. Without it, you stay stuck. Yes, those years were full of challenges, but also self-discovery. It makes me think that our lives are a collection of lessons, and we were made to make choices that teach us about who we are and what path we need to be on. I realize now that if I am not listening to myself, I'm not on the right path, and my life fills with unnecessary stress. It sounds so simple, but sometimes when you spend years stuffing that voice down, as I did for so long, it is replaced with fear and stress — you can't hear your own voice anymore. You become lost and stuck; to hear it again, a transformation needs to happen. Like a shell wedged in the sand, you need to dig it up and shake it off to see its true features.

WAKING UP TO WHAT IS KEEPING ME DOWN

After my cancer diagnosis, my journey to self-discovery has been a mix of research, keeping my mind open, new experiences, and sharing thoughts with others. I have read so much about stress and the effects it has on the body over time. Chronic stress can speed up the spread of cancer throughout the body. When the body becomes stressed, neurotransmitters are released, stimulating cancer cells.

The importance of reducing stress was explained to me by my oncologist, my cancer specialist, and even many of my friends who know me best, but it wasn't until I was in a conversation with my last living aunt, Mary, that it really hit home. As mentioned earlier, my grandmother was 65 when she passed from breast cancer, but my grandmother's older sister, my great-aunt Marjorie, was in her 90s when she passed. She had undergone a mastectomy as well but had lived a much longer life. When I shared this with my aunt, she explained that my grandmother had lived a very stressful life. I am sure my Aunt Marjorie had many stressful times in her life, but she didn't live with chronic stress like my grandmother. It was eye-opening to me. I need to find a different way to live if I want to live a full life.

Chronic stress and feelings of anxiety have become so familiar to me, but I didn't notice the damage it was actually doing. Once you become aware of it, you can feel the effects on the body. My chest tightens when I think of all the things in my life that aren't working. My daily thoughts are all about survival. I am easily overwhelmed and have difficulty sleeping and concentrating. My thoughts are sometimes rapid and disorganized with deep feelings of a loss of control, which lead to feeling helpless. I wake up many times in the middle of the night worried about paying my bills, or something important I forgot to do. My whole body pounds and vibrates, my heart thumping so hard it feels like it could jump out of my chest. Sometimes I get up and do jumping jacks and pushups to try to make it stop, because when I sit in my bed just thinking about my worries, the feelings are more intense.

For advice on how to cope better, I have turned to professionals, healers, my online support group, research, and those in my life who understand the impact. Sure, stress cannot be avoided in life. Short-lived feelings of stress are a regular part of daily life. It's when these feelings become chronic or long-lasting that they can severely impact your health.

Once I came to the realization that stress is a big part of getting cancer, and the real possibility of it causing cancer to return or spread, I began to focus every day on shifting my thoughts to a more positive mindset. I have made a very conscious shift to move towards things that bring me joy and away from the things that cause me stress.

This isn't always easy for me to do. I have been a full-time single mother for a long time, and the circumstances have me feeling stuck some days. My ADHD makes many things more complicated than they have to be. I have to plan my days out so I am remembering to take my supplements and prepare food so I am eating right and taking care of my body. But my biggest struggles have been finding jobs that don't put too much pressure on my daily life and have flexibility so I can plan for doctor's appointments and activities that allow me to put my health first, all while paying the bills and keeping our home afloat until my children are through school and ready to begin their fully independent lives.

Yes, the struggle is real. I still have challenges and insecurities, but I acknowledge those things for what they are and I don't let them hold me back. I found ways to tone down the chronic stress. I started doing more of the things I enjoy. I walk outside every day, rain or shine. I use that time to talk to friends who are uplifting and listen to podcasts that inspire me. I have learned to use my breath to settle my body whenever the feelings of anxiety and stress emerge, and I take the time for self-care to heal my body and soul. I began to develop a plan to work towards having my own business again by using my creative gifts.

The simple fact is, having cancer woke me up and made me look at my life in such a different way. The biggest shift of all has been in my mindset. I focus on feeling grateful, even in the small moments that may have seemed insignificant in the past. There are small gifts surrounding us every day; we just need to be open to noticing them. That small shift in perception can be magical.

GO LIVE LIFE

Cancer seems to be in the rearview mirror now, but health scares still emerge. Recently, I've had sensations in my head and ears, so my oncologist ordered an MRI of my brain. The findings were worrisome, especially when they come to you in scary medical language. When I was able to see the neurologist a few weeks later, the news was far better than I imagined. He told me not to worry and to "Go Live Life."

He was right; I could choose to spend my days worrying about things out of my control, or I could embrace every day like the gift that it is. Whatever our struggles are, we have the ability to move through them — whether we believe it or not some days. And we can choose how we see our world.

I am ready for this new chapter. Each day, I'm learning to find and follow my inner voice. With a lot of practice, I'm managing my stress, and I keep looking for the lessons in the journey.

Now is the time for me to finally "Go Live Life!" The life I was meant to live.

Robin Pawlak Garstka is a devoted mom to two sons, a sister, a daughter, a loyal friend, a dog lover, and a graphic designer (not necessarily in that order). She is a nature enthusiast and an artist at the core of all she sees and does. She loves spending her time outside in New England, and at the end of the day, you can find her chasing a good sunset.

If you would like to get in touch with Robin, she can be reached at robingarstka@gmail.com and on Instagram @rgcreatively

ABOUT JENNIFER GULBRAND
& SHEBREATHES

soul stories

Jennifer Gulbrand is an Author, Speaker, Trauma-Informed Somatic Therapy Practitioner, Embodiment Coach, Spiritual Mentor, Holistic Healer and Podcast Host (High Vibes + Grateful Heart).

She is a self-proclaimed "Corporate Dropout Gone Goddess" who discovered her life purpose as a builder of heart-centered communities and safe, supportive containers holding space for growth and healing. She founded SheBreathes Balance Women's Collaborative and the WeBreathe Wellness Center to help raise the collective vibration and heal the human heart, one beautiful soul at a time.

Jenn's passion is empowering women to stand up, speak out, and live in better alignment with their true nature. She walks her talk when it comes to lifting other people up to help them shine their own unique light into the world, and this book is a testament to her commitment.

She facilitates individual and group coaching sessions, leads business+mindset masterminds, teaches workshops, offers retreats, and shares her insight as a speaker at women's education and empowerment conferences. She combines positive psychology, mindfulness, meditation, breath work, movement, integrated energy, and vibrational sound healing to improve people's overall wellbeing and return them to a state of balance and alignment.

Jenn has recently founded the WeBreathe WellBeing Soul Sanctuary, a 501(c)(3) nonprofit. Its mission is to provide a safe, supportive container for growth and healing, with programs and services designed to cultivate human connection, a sense of belonging, and a commitment of service to the world. The Soul Sanctuary is seeking funding support to secure their own location to cultivate immersive retreat experiences, in natural surroundings, for individuals and groups to gather in unity with a shared intention to raise the collective consciousness and directly combat the effects of a global mental health crisis.

Learn about Jenn and her work at www.jenngulbrand.com and follow her on Instagram @IamJennGulbrand.

Learn about WeBreathe Wellness Center at *www.webreathewellness.com* and follow us at Instagram @webreathewellness

Learn more about SheBreathes Balance Women's Collaborative at *www.shebreathesbalance.com* and follow us at Instagram @shebreathesbalance

Learn about WeBreathe WellBeing Soul Sanctuary, 501(c)(3) at *www.webreathewellbeingsoulsanctuary.org* and follow us on Instagram @wbwbsoulsanctuary

ACKNOWLEDGEMENTS

I am immensely grateful to everyone who contributed to the creation of the SheBreathes Soul Stories Collection, both directly and indirectly. Their support, inspiration and guidance have been invaluable.

I want to express my deepest appreciation to our editor, Beth Knaus, whose dedication, expertise, and keen eye transformed this collection from an idea into its best possible form. Her insight and attention to detail elevated every aspect of the process.

We are all indebted to our portrait photographer, Robin Ganter, who captured the true essence of our 22 contributing authors. She made the experience fun while creating a safe, nurturing space for each woman's true beauty to shine.

And, as always, I wish to share my heartfelt gratitude to our book designer, Robin Garstka, whose creative vision and design expertise breathed life into the cover and interior pages of the book. Her artistic sensibilities gave the work a visual identity to perfectly complement the content.

And special thanks to Dave Pasquantonio, who guided us through the final stages of the book production process. We could not have gotten to the finish line without him.

This collection of soul stories stands as a testament to the power of collaboration and the richness of diverse perspectives. I am immensely grateful to the 22 contributing authors who have generously shared their insights, experiences, and creativity to make this project a reality. Each of you brought a unique voice to the pages of the book, enriching its content and sparking conscious and meaningful conversations. Your dedication and commitment to our shared vision had everything to do with the power of our co-creation.

This collection is a culmination of the efforts of many, and I am humbled by your support. Thank you all for being a part of this incredible journey.

With deep appreciation,

Jennifer

Made in the USA
Middletown, DE
10 November 2023

42251670R00159